Quiet Water
New Jersey:
Canoe & Kayak Guide

Kathy Kenley

APPALACHIAN MOUNTAIN CLUB BOOKS
BOSTON, MASSACHUSETTS

Cover photograph: Kindra Clineff
Cover & book design: Carol Bast Tyler

Distributed by The Globe Pequot Press, Inc., Guilford, CT

Library of Congress Cataloging-in-Publication Data is available.

The paper used in this publication meets the minimum requirements of
the American National Standard for Information Sciences—Permanence of Paper for Printed Library Materials, ANSI Z39.48–1984.

**Due to changes in conditions
use of the information in this book
is at the sole risk of the user.**

Printed on recycled paper using soy-based inks.

Printed in the United States of America.

10 9 8 7 6 5 4 3 2 1   01 02 03 04 05 06

Contents

Northern New Jersey

To my mother

Acknowledgments

First and foremost, I would like to thank the AMC for the opportunity to write this book and enjoy paddling many new sites in the process. My thanks go to Beth Krusi, editor, for her guidance and kind words along the way: her patience and understanding are appreciated.

Many people I met during this adventure helped me by supplying information about various sites and their surroundings. The list would be too long to singly name and thank all the park rangers, police officers, anglers, birders, and naturalists who gave their assistance. I met many local kayakers, canoeists, and anglers who extended their time and gave me information about their favorite places.

A special thanks to Professor Jack Connor of The Richard Stockton College of New Jersey, who not only helped review the introductory text material, but gave me continual encouragement in writing about nature. My appreciation also goes to his colleague, Professor Mike Hozik, for his guidance in assembling the geologic history of the area and reviewing the final product.

I am deeply indebted to many friends: Karen Roseman who spent countless hours drawing many of the site maps and helped with general research; Fran Orlofsky and Ted Ellis who helped proofread site descriptions; and Mike Kelly who helped with site investigations. I thank Bill Bell, of Bel Haven Canoe and Kayak, who provided valuable information on local wildlife. I extend appreciation to my kayaking friends who accompanied me on numerous trips and made them enjoyable, helping uncover information and giving encouragement throughout the project. This list includes Karen Roseman, Fran Orlofsky, Bill Bell, Linda Burdett, Gerard Marcus, Mike Kelly, Fred ("Fritz") Mitchel, and Mark Rogers.

Finally, warm love and appreciation go to my mother who encouraged my interest in nature from an early age instead of making me play with dolls. Thanks, Mom.

Introduction

Most kids have a magnetic attraction to water, as evidenced by the number of puddles they'll go out of their way to jump in. Some of us never outgrow this attraction.

Something intangible, almost spiritual, happens when I place my boat on the water. Sitting quietly for a moment, I let the water's soothing bob realign my soul. I dip my paddle over the side and the little splash starts my transport on a magic liquid carpet ride. I watch an osprey hunt for fish or listen to the symphony of avian songs that makes me feel one with nature.

Other than some canoe experiences I had as a child in the Pocono Mountains of Pennsylvania, my paddling adventures began in my late teens when I stumbled across an old, small kayak at a garage sale. It was light enough to load and unload myself and, more importantly, it fit on the roof of my small car without extending past the bumpers—well, at least not too far. A strange sense of freedom came with that first boat, a freedom rimmed with both the excitement of adventure and the peacefulness of solitude. Opening local county maps, my eyes zoomed in on every splotch of blue; the search was on for the magic blue liquid.

Among my favorite places are quiet lakes, marshes, ponds, and slow-moving streams, where I can sit on the water and drink in the scenery and wildlife with all my senses. Seeing what animals live in this little cove or what might be found around the back of that island tweaks my curiosity. With each new site, I discover different habitats and learn the links between ecosystems—their similarities and their differences. As a naturalist, my binoculars, camera, field guides, and a journal usually accompany me.

One tactic I occasionally employ is to combine biking and paddling. I lock my bike to a tree on the downstream take-out of a waterway or the opposite end of the lake, then go to the put-in and start paddling. At the end of the trip, I lock up the boat, bike back to my vehicle, and drive back to pick up the boat. The bike rides range from 15 to 40 minutes, and it's a great way to see an area's land and water views and get an upper and lower body workout on the same outing. A few such trips are included in this book, although it is not necessary to take a bike along to enjoy these waters.

Why Quiet Waters?

When the opportunity to prepare this book for the Appalachian Mountain Club (AMC) arose, I gladly accepted it, to seek out new sites and visit those I hadn't paddled in years. Available books only covered the many rivers that dissect the state, but none mentioned the hundreds of lakes, ponds, and reservoirs available to paddlers. Open skies over large bodies of water draw a different variety of wildlife, like osprey, eagles, ducks, and certain hawks, which do not frequent narrow streams or rivers. These quiet waters offer their own special ambiance, one suited to those who enjoy the tranquility of nature or want a respite, however brief, from hectic city life.

Livery services are necessary for trips down a river and are not conducive to picking up and paddling whenever you please, particularly if you prefer going solo. The serenity of lazily paddling in the middle of a lake, watching and listening to wildlife, is lost if you're being swept downstream by a current. During summer months, local rivers overflow with kayaks, canoes, and tubes, more reminiscent of an amusement park bumper-car ride than a pristine river. But on hot weekends at busier lakes, it isn't too difficult to find a peaceful area to enjoy. Quiet waters also are ideal for families taking children out for the first time, when a trip may need to end earlier than planned. Novices can gain experience on the calm and unthreatening environment of lakes and ponds. As an experienced paddler, I visit a small local pond a few times each spring just to check out my equipment and practice different strokes and maneuvers before venturing out on longer paddles.

The Selection Process

What's the recipe for a book such as this? Take a couple of weeks pouring over detailed county and topographical maps, thousands of road miles, a few hundred water miles, 15-plus rolls of film, a dozen small notepads, lots of camp food, and mix well. My culinary skills did not improve, but my repertoire of paddling sites escalated ten-fold. Along the way I learned how to put my minivan into "squeeze gear" on narrow roads and teased it into becoming four-wheel drive for short distances. We have some absolutely delightful gems within the state that I encourage all who read this book to visit. If you don't, you'll be missing some of the best paddling adventures in the Northeast. Of the more than 140 sites investigated, 51 locations (70 lakes and ponds) were selected for inclusion.

How did I make selections for this book? My main focus was to provide information on the better sites available throughout the state to assist those just getting started and increase the repertoire of more experienced paddlers. After consulting with my regular paddling buddies, I also made it a goal to have a wide enough geographic selection of sites to provide a location within 45 minutes of anyone, from the beginner who wishes to get out frequently for experience, to a parent initiating their child into the sport, to someone who simply cannot travel longer distances. To that end, a few sites have been included that may seem less than ideal for the more experienced paddler out for a full day on wilderness waters.

Obviously, some counties have an abundance of lakes. A few counties could have taken a solid month to investigate every body of water larger than 20 acres, but this book would never have been finished. Where lake density was thick, I tried to choose the best body of water, not necessarily the biggest or the most popular. Other counties exhibited a paucity of selection due to lack of topography or inaccessibility. I kept a record of every site visited, including those rejected and listed a reason for their exclusion. Try as I might, I didn't quite attain my personal goal of a site within 45 minutes of anyone, but I came close.

If you're out for the quietest paddling, select sites offering only boating, fishing, and possibly camping; swimming, picnicking, and recreational facilities tend to draw large crowds, particularly in July and August. If the whole family is out for the day, and you are the only one who paddles, you will want sites that provide additional recreational activities for the family to enjoy. What each of us looks for on any given day is different—some days it's a long, silent paddle; other days we just need something big enough to float our boat. The trip highlights chart will help guide you to the sites that meet your needs.

Equipment

Any book on paddling must have sections on equipment, technique, and safety. For those of you who are experienced paddlers, please take a moment to review these sections. For those just starting to paddle, I offer only preliminary tips and advice, as numerous books detail equipment, paddling techniques, and boat styles far better than I can in an abbreviated format.

Four necessary pieces of equipment are: a canoe or kayak, an appropriate paddle, a first-aid kit, and a personal floatation device (PFD). I would add to that a whistle and a hand bilge pump or a large boat sponge.

If you're old enough, you remember a time when there were only two types of sneakers: Converse high-tops or regular. Today sneaker designs exist for every sport and then some. The same is true for kayaks and canoes to some degree. There are styles for whitewater, rodeo, sea, surf, touring, and racing, which can set even the more experienced paddler's head spinning. Don't let the endless styles overwhelm you. Since your main interest is paddling quiet waters, you'll want a boat that is stable and tracks well. If you intend to camp or carry extensive camera equipment, make sure the volume of the boat is large enough to carry the desired gear. Your best bet is to rent a boat a few times until you get the feel of paddling and are comfortable. Outfitters gladly recommend models they feel will best suit your needs and your physical characteristics such as height and weight. When you're ready to buy, find a boat that handles well for your current skill level—you can always upgrade later.

Dealers located near a lake usually let you test paddle different models for little or no fee. Paddle fests held late spring through early fall offer a great opportunity to try out a number of boats. Some rental operations offer end-of-season sales on used boats—a great way to pick up a boat inexpensively. Most of all, make sure you're comfortable in the boat.

Materials also vary. Roto-molded plastic is the least expensive and best for beginners, as it takes quite a bit of abuse. Fiberglass increases the cost tremendously and, although the boat will move faster than its plastic counterpart, is more susceptible to damage from rocks or gravelly bottoms. Plastic and fiberglass models are comparable in weight and occupy the heavier side of the spectrum. Kevlar increases the cost but decreases weight substantially. Carbon fiber is the lightest and most expensive but is more susceptible to damage.

Camera and binoculars add to the enjoyment of wildlife observation, but they should be kept in waterproof bags, also referred to as dry bags, until ready for use. Dry bags come in a variety of sizes suitable for anything from a small camera to a tent. I keep a small dry bag in the cockpit of my kayak for items frequently used such as sunscreen, sunglasses, camera, guidebooks, and binoculars. Another dry bag behind the seat carries extra clothes in case the day turns chilly or wet.

Always take plenty of water if you intend to be on the water for any length of time. The heat of a summer's day or the dry west winds of fall can bring on dehydration. And how about a small journal? Not only is it a log for sites paddled but also a reference for wildlife observations and friends you've paddled with or met along the way. A change of clothes and a towel kept in your boat are handy just in case you get caught in a rainstorm or have an otherwise soggy trip.

If you plan to visit sites where you have to carry your boat any distance, wheeled carts and canoe yokes are available. The carts are compact and fold up to store neatly in the bottom of your boat. Wash all your gear with clean, fresh water at the end of a trip and dry thoroughly to prevent corrosion and mold.

Technique

Unlike whitewater or ocean paddling, quiet water requires no special skills, but knowing how to hold a paddle correctly and properly execute the basic forward, backward, sideway (draw), and turning strokes will make for a more enjoyable day. It's always better to learn correct technique initially than to correct sloppy habits later.

If you can, find the time to take a quick lesson. Most outfitters offer private and group instruction for beginning and experienced paddlers. A half-hour to one hour lesson is all you need to start off in the right direction. Novices should stay with smaller ponds before tackling large lakes, where wind and waves could challenge them beyond their capabilities. Most lakes are usually glasslike in the early morning hours, but as an old salt once told me, "As the sun comes up, so does the wind." That adage holds true for the ocean and the lake down the street.

For those of you who have some experience, continue to refine current skills and add new ones. Braces and self-rescue techniques should be learned prior to venturing out to the middle of a large lake or reservoir. Take a few minutes to review these skills at the beginning and periodically throughout your paddling season. You may never need them, but if a squall arises suddenly or a large boat passes dangerously close, you will be prepared. Increasing your skill level will not only make you feel more comfortable with your boat, but will instill a level of confidence in case less-than-ideal conditions arise—and they eventually will.

Basic navigation skills come in handy on larger lakes, where rainstorms or fog can obscure the shoreline suddenly. (Most prevalent in early morning and late afternoon during spring and fall, fog is due to a marked difference between land and air temperatures.) Always bring a compass and know how to use it properly.

Safety

The single most important piece of safety equipment is the personal floatation device (PFD), also called a life jacket or life vest, with a waterproof whistle attached. The PFD should always be worn, because even the most experienced paddlers can find themselves on the wrong side of the waterline. Some lakes and reservoirs require a PFD be worn at all times or be readily accessible within 30 seconds. Don the vest immediately if fog, inclement weather, or other hazardous conditions arise. Nonswimmers and children should *always* wear a PFD, with straps secured tightly enough to prevent the vest from slipping off. Children should not wear an adult PFD, as they can easily slip out of it; make sure they have a child's vest with a crotch strap that fits properly.

Unless you have a propensity for a particular color or feel you must make a fashion statement, select a yellow or orange PFD, particularly for children or nonswimmers. Light colors are seen more readily against a dark water surface, facilitating quicker rescue. PFDs also add a bit of warmth on chilly days. Small children riding in a canoe or in the front compartment of a tandem (two-person) kayak should be warned not to lean over the side, stand up, or move about suddenly.

Motorboats over ten horsepowers are loud and can be unsettling to novice paddlers as they zip by throwing large wakes. If caught

Two friends check each other's vest straps for snugness.

unexpectedly, turn the bow of your boat into the wake as quickly as possible to prevent swamping. Most waters listed in this book either do not permit motors or impose a maximum speed of ten horsepowers. Fortunately, many lakes ban personal watercrafts altogether, and more than one lake bans their use on weekends during the summer. Wildlife Management Areas, except for Union and Prospertown Lakes, prohibit gasoline motors. In addition, many bodies of water are located within or adjacent to prime hunting areas. Check with your local state Fish and Game official or local sporting goods store for specific hunting seasons, particularly in spring and fall.

Water robs the body of heat 25 times faster than air, potentially causing a condition called hypothermia, or subnormal body temperature. Drowning may occur when extended immersion in cold water cools the body to such a degree that a person becomes physically and mentally incapacitated. Symptoms of hypothermia include slurred speech, loss of coordination, confusion, apathy, and irrational behavior; all symptoms become more critical when you are paddling solo. Prime conditions for hypothermia exist in spring and early summer, when water temperatures are cold but warm air lulls us into wearing less-than-adequate clothing for coldwater immersion. Roll up your long-sleeved shirt if you must, but don't take it off. Should you accidentally upset your boat, put your PFD on immediately and roll down those sleeves. A PFD not only adds a small amount of insulation, but will also keep you afloat should you lose consciousness. Change into warm, dry clothes as soon as practical and drink warm liquids. Pick up a pamphlet on hypothermia from your local hospital or American Red Cross chapter to learn more.

If you paddle solo, let someone know where you are going, especially if you live alone. In big-boat arenas, it's called a float plan. Recently, a very experienced friend who lives alone went kayaking down a local river swollen with recent rains. He hit a submerged log, quickly found himself inspecting the river bottom, and surfaced with his head just inches from a fat overhanging tree limb. "I could have been knocked unconscious and nobody would have known where I was!" he said. "And the water was cold—I could have gone hypothermic." We discussed the incident among our circle of paddling friends, promising to send an e-mail or call someone whenever we go out alone, and let them know when we return.

Taking the Children Along

Paddling with children is rewarding but requires special considerations. In addition to wearing a PFD, impress on them the importance of proper movement while in a boat such as moving slowly without sudden moves, sitting and staying low in the boat, and knowing the proper procedure for entering and exiting the boat. Plan on shorter trips initially. Long paddles may require you to land occasionally and let them romp around a bit, even if the space is small, depending on the child's normal activity level. Most children are so excited to be going out in a boat that they sit quietly and absorb the sights and sounds—at least the first few times out.

Try to include them in the adventure. Play games that involve spotting specific turtles or birds. Ask their opinion on which way to go, or what they think about the scenery in a particular cove. Inexpensive binoculars or a disposable camera will help engage them in nature observations. Having some equipment to call their own, and being responsible for it, will help make them feel part of the trip. Very young children may want to bring along a special toy, perhaps a small one that won't get ruined if it gets wet.

Kids eat—often! Be sure to pack enough snacks and drinks for the paddle as well as for the trip home. Pack an extra sweater or jacket for them, even in summer, as a light breeze over cool mountain waters or in dense shade near shore can be chilly for those not paddling. A change of clothes kept in the car will be handy if they accidentally trip and fall into the water getting in or out of the boat.

Something happens when they get between eight and ten years old —they want to paddle; not just hold a paddle, but be part of the actual process. Child-sized canoe and kayak paddles are available, and if you want to keep the peace and avert mutiny, buy one. Keeping kids in a tandem kayak while they're learning techniques only works for a short time. Once they get the hang of it, they'll want their own kayak. In canoes, you'll be able to stretch this out a little longer by teaching them both bow and stern techniques before they can adequately handle their own boat. Enjoy the experience of sharing this wonderful world with children.

Wildlife

It's a well-known practice by wildlife photographers, birders, and other serious nature observers that once you are in an area of abundant wildlife, sit still. Let them come to you, and you have a better chance of closer observation for longer periods of time. Dawn and dusk are the best times to spot deer, raccoons, otter, and other mammals that come to drink water. Look for animal tracks near tiny openings around the lakes they frequent, get into position ahead of time, and then wait quietly and patiently for their arrival.

Do not feed wildlife and *never* attempt to touch or approach wild animals. Raccoons, bears, skunk, fox, and coyotes are potential visitors to your campsite and may be encountered while hiking, particularly in the mountainous northern regions. Raccoons and bears have been known to open coolers and rummage through food containers; keep food tightly packed and stored in your vehicle or away from the campsite—never in your tent. Clean all cooking implements immediately after use, and place garbage where animals cannot smell it or gain access to it.

Any wild animal can harbor diseases such as rabies. Never approach or chase after an animal; you can disrupt its daily routine and frighten it into defending itself or its territory. In addition, never get between a wild animal and its young. If you accidentally find yourself in this situation, lower your eyes and back away slowly. Should you be bitten or scratched accidentally, seek medical attention immediately.

Jersey, along with other Mid-Atlantic and New England states, is home to *Ixodes scapularis*, the deer tick that carries the bacteria responsible for Lyme disease. This tick normally crawls around on the body for three or more hours before settling on a spot. It takes another hour or two before burrowing deep into the skin. While you do have plenty of time before a tick can do damage, it is wise to check yourself often if you brush past foliage while loading or unloading your boat. Always do a thorough check for ticks at the end of the day.

Tick kits, available at most outdoor and sporting goods stores, contain a small magnifying glass, specialized tweezers, and instructions on proper removal, as well as common signs and symptoms of Lyme disease. A bulls-eye rash, the most obvious sign, often develops within a day or two around the bite, but not everyone is lucky enough to develop that symptom. Lyme disease is easily treated if detected early.

Fishing, Crabbing, and Permits

Catching your own dinner, whether camping overnight or returning home, is a rewarding experience. If you are camping, bring along some add-water-and-heat meals—just in case the fish are not biting that day. Break-apart rods that come in two or three sections are relatively inexpensive and stow compactly in even the smallest boat. Rod-holders are available for canoes and kayaks.

Blue crabs, at their peak in August, can be caught in brackish coastal regions from late June through September. Crabbing requires no license, but current state law requires a legal minimum size of 4.5 inches across the body, tip to tip.

Be advised that anyone between the ages of 16 and 69 must have and display a valid New Jersey fishing license to fish New Jersey's fresh waters. Licenses may be obtained from most county or municipal offices or agents, such as sporting goods stores and bait shops. Year-round resident and nonresident licenses are available as are two- and seven-day licenses. Special licenses are available for senior residents (age 65 and older). To obtain a resident license, you must have lived in New Jersey for six months immediately prior to the time of application. If you are a New Jersey resident 70 years of age or older, no fishing license is required but you must carry acceptable proof of age, such as a driver's license.

Geography

Although New Jersey is small, its geography and geology provide a diversity of ecosystems within relatively short distances of each other. Crystal clear mountain lakes, salt- and freshwater marshes, sweet cedar swamps, and hardwood forests each offer their own special scenery and wildlife.

New Jersey is a peninsula, attached to the North American continent by a 50-mile-wide strip along its northern border, shared with New York. It is bounded on the far northeast by the Hudson River, on the east by the Atlantic Ocean, on the west by the Delaware River, and on the south/southwest by the brackish Delaware Bay. Along the Atlantic coast, numerous barrier islands offer protection from storm waves for populated towns on the mainland coast. Temperatures vary slightly between the northern and southern parts of the state, with the southern coastal region being the warmest. In winter the ameliorating effect of the Atlantic Ocean along the coast contrasts with the chilly heights of the northern mountains. During much of the summer, ocean breezes help cool coastal regions.

If you mention the Appalachian Mountains to someone, chances are that most will imagine the mountainous states of Virginia, West Virginia, and Pennsylvania; yet the Appalachian Ridge and Valley Region can be seen in the northwest corner of New Jersey. A flat coastal plain, some may find mundane, comprises more than half the state's land. Go to a brackish pond or back bay where various shore birds can be seen, then visit the rusty, tannin-stained waters of a cedar swamp and you'll find two very different environments.

A Brief Lesson in Geology

The earth is a living planet, undergoing daily change. Its outer surface, or crust, is broken up into plates, which move about the surface at seemingly imperceptible rates of four centimeters per year on average. These miniscule year-to-year movements over millions and millions of years have produced large changes in the landscape.

Plates basically do three things: collide, break apart, or slide past each other. When plates collide, some of the land between is crumpled and uplifted, creating mountain ranges like the Appalachians and the Sierra Nevadas.

A different process occurs when a large plate or landmass breaks apart, creating two smaller plates. This is going on today in East Africa in an area called the Great Rift Valley, which possesses the greatest rupture on the earth's land surface and one of the few features visible from space. Given another ten million years or so, Africa's landmass will probably occupy two separate plates.

When plates slide past one another and tension built up along that boundary is suddenly released, earthquakes occur. The example most Americans are familiar with is the San Andreas Fault, where the Pacific plate is sliding past the North American plate as it has done for millions of years. Some readers probably remember the 1989 Loma Prieta earthquake that occurred during the World Series in Oakland, California, a city situated along the San Andreas Fault.

About 550 million years ago, a huge landmass began to rift in a jagged pattern, which would eventually form the edges of the present-day African and North American plates. A few crumbs broke off during

Appalachian Ridge and Valley Region

Piedmont Plateau

Atlantic Coastal Plain

New Jersey

rifting, leaving behind smaller landmasses. Volcanic ridges formed as the crust thinned over a long period of time. Before the rifting was complete, the two large parts of the original landmass began moving back toward each other. One of the small landmasses in between, called the Piedmont, was thrust onto the margin of the North American side resulting in the formation of the ancestral Appalachian Mountains around 500 million years ago. As those mountains eroded, rain and wind carried small particles south and southeast toward the sea, creating the base of a low-lying coastal plain. During that time, Africa was still moving closer to North America.

Over the next 300 million years, global events allowed the sea to advance and retreat several times over the lower elevations, each time leaving behind saltwater sediments along with some of the animals that inhabited those shallow seas. Finally, around 250 million years ago, Africa collided with North America, compressing, folding, and uplifting the lands in between in a mountain-building event that created the present-day Appalachians. While the Appalachians extend from Newfoundland to South Carolina, the brunt of the impact took place between New York and southern Maryland, creating a series of wrinkles in the land roughly parallel to our continental edge. Today we refer to that prominent system of land features as the Appalachian Ridge and Valley Region. Folded layers of rocks are visible in many roadcuts throughout the northern part of the state. (Do not examine them while driving!) Shallow ocean sediments also were lifted onto the land, and today fossil-hunting enthusiasts find remnants of those ancient seas, from Bound Brook in central New Jersey to High Point in the extreme northwest corner.

About 200 million years ago, Africa and North America began to separate again and, as rifting progressed, volcanic activity started that would eventually form the Watchung and Orange Mountains and the Palisades Sill. This volcanic activity lasted 500,000 years, but the breakup wasn't complete until about 180 million years ago. Bit by bit, the new mountains started eroding; wind and rain carried sediments eastward in a process that continues today.

Within the past few hundred thousand years, in a period known as the Wisconsin Ice Age, ice sheets advanced and retreated several times over North America, occasionally reaching as far south as Trenton. Though the last Ice Age ended 10,000 to 12,000 years ago, it left its mark on the terrain. Each time the ice advanced, glaciers carved broad valleys, scoured and gouged the land, and grounded down the mountains. When the climate warmed and the glaciers retreated, meltwater washed particles of sand and gravel previously locked within the ice sheet to the south and southeast. Today hundreds of feet of that sand and gravel form the top layers of land in the southern half of New Jersey. Occasionally glaciers would pick up large chunks of rock and transport them within the ice sheet. After the ice melted, these rocks, called erratics, were left behind, often tens of miles from their original sources.

With the exception of recent glacial and volcanic activities, humans were not around during the events that shaped the earth's landforms. Today, geologists examine the workings of present-day processes and combine this knowledge with evidence from rocks to develop theories about when the geologic process happened.

What to Expect in New Jersey

New Jersey lies in the highly populated Northeast corridor between two major cities: Philadelphia and New York City. Let's not kid ourselves. We cannot expect to find as many remote areas per square mile as in Maine or Montana within our borders, but we do have many beautiful bodies of water to paddle, some are quite isolated. I have discovered many lakes in more "remote" regions extremely crowded and unappealing—houses line the shores down to the water's edge, while motorboats and personal watercrafts roil the waters like a storm. Other places are rimmed with private property, or are noted as "township residents only," depriving public access. In contrast, some lakes and ponds within highly populated towns proved a very lovely surprise, with dense woods surrounding some or all of the lake and private houses set well back from its banks. A few of these lakes had only a narrow, landscaped swath surrounding them, sometimes with meandering biking and walking trails, but they were still a pleasant oasis in the midst of a large urban setting.

We don't have bumper stickers from New Jersey that read, "This car climbed Mount So-And-So." What mountains we do have in the northwestern quadrant of the state are small, with 1,804 feet High Point Mountain in High Point State Park being the greatest elevation in the state. Yet within these mountains are some absolutely delightful pristine lakes beset with islands and interesting coves.

In the flat coastal plain of southern New Jersey, Apple Pie Hill rises meekly to a whopping 183 feet above sea level. If it weren't for the damming of rivers in this region, I doubt there would be any lakes deep enough to paddle. In reality, most New Jersey lakes and ponds have been dammed to some degree, increasing their holding capacity and acreage for recreational use or irrigation. Reservoirs, of course, are waterways dammed expressly for use in times of drought, even though they may have been a large lake initially.

Since more than half the state is a low-lying coastal plain bordering the Atlantic Ocean and Delaware Bay, you'll find a number of sites in tidal saltwater and brackish marshes carefully chosen for their minimal current. Although first-timers have paddled these waters with no problem, I strongly advise gaining some experience on other waters first. It is equally important to know tide schedules. Starting your trip against the current while you are still fresh and letting it help you on the way back is best. Make your first trips short, until you get the feel of tidal currents for that particular waterway. These habitats contain extensive wildlife, making it well worth the effort.

You and the Environment

The more often you get out to enjoy the ponds and lakes of New Jersey, the more you will appreciate our precious ecosystems and understand the need to help protect them. Numerous community organizations, college clubs, and paddling clubs host cleanups of various waterways. They are usually well advertised and paddlers can join in the effort. Perhaps in the future you could organize an annual cleanup of your favorite location. On an individual level, my friends and I often carry a trash bag with us to remove carelessly discarded refuse. It may be a small effort, but it makes the waters cleaner for everyone and safer for wildlife. It's a good idea to carry a trash bag or two in your vehicle anyway, as many sites lack refuse containers, having a "carry-in, carry-out" policy instead. Books such as *Soft Paths* offer a wide variety of tips for hikers and campers to minimize their impact on and help to protect and preserve our environment. For more information on minimizing your impact on our natural resources, contact Leave No Trace at 800-332-4100 or www.LNT.org (see page 195).

New Jersey Audubon Society acquires and maintains wildlife sanctuaries that protect wildlife and natural habitats, and educational centers that foster environmental awareness. The society currently maintains seven major sanctuaries and is responsible in part for 22 others. Many of its on-premises programs and community-sponsored events are perfect for the younger generation. The Nature Conservancy places its emphasis on the identification and preservation of ecologically important areas and endangered species. Look to the Sierra Club for involvement with environmental concerns and to join organized hikes sponsored around the state.

The Appalachian Mountain Club (AMC) fosters public awareness of environmental and conservation issues through its books, publications, and workshops while promoting enjoyment of outdoor recreational activities with minimal impact. With protection of our ecosystems at the forefront, the AMC has spearheaded numerous conservation programs and has helped cofound several organizations. The AMC Mohican Outdoor Center, located in the 70,000-acre Delaware Water Gap National Recreation Area, is a great base for outdoor exploration in New Jersey. Check out the AMC website, www.outdoors.org, for more information.

The New York/New Jersey Trail Conference, based in Manhattan, maintains more than 1,000 miles of trails in two states, and monitors 7,600 acres of National Park Service lands that are part of the Appalachian Trail system. Its water-resistant trail maps are conveniently sized for backpacking or paddling. The goal of the New Jersey Division of Fish and Wildlife is to protect habitats necessary to maintain species diversity and wildlife distribution, while at the same time balancing commercial and recreational interests.

What a thrill it was to see tax dollars and voter opinions at work through the state-sponsored Green Acres Program, which provides loans and grants to various governmental agencies and nonprofit organizations in order to purchase properties and develop them into parks. The list is too long to enumerate every site where parklands were due completely or in part to this program. To date, the Green Acres Program has helped preserve almost half a million acres, and the numbers keep climbing.

You should keep abreast of land around lakes purchased through such agencies as Green Acres, The Nature Conservancy, the New Jersey

Division of Fish and Wildlife, and others that open up lakes to public access. Pay attention to election day issues such as bond referendums allocating funds to acquire lands for preservation. Whatever we can do to help protect and preserve our environment also will ensure that we have scenic waters to paddle and wildlife to observe. (See the Appendix on page 188 for more information about the organizations mentioned above.)

How to Use This Book

Each site includes a description of the lake and surrounding area, directions for getting there, a basic map showing roads and launch areas, and what you can expect to see. Campgrounds come and campgrounds go; for that reason, only those available within the premises of the lake property have been noted. For up-to-date information, it is best to purchase a campground guide. Suggested books are listed in the Appendix on page 187.

Maps and directions in this book are for near-site use only. Complement a large state map with county maps for finer detail, which becomes important in urban areas. County maps are also handy in backcountry areas, where route signs may not be displayed at reasonable intervals or properly indicated at critical junctions.

Backcountry roads also have a habit of changing names at every little hamlet and junction to further confuse matters. A topographic map book, such as that produced by DeLorme and others, not only shows topographic features, but many unimproved roads not indicated on county maps. Topographic maps of individual quadrangles are the best for exploring remote areas. They show almost all unimproved roads and trails, one of which may provide the only access to a new pond (for map sources, see the Appendix on page 186).

Various state parks, particularly those with recreational facilities, charge an entrance fee from Memorial Day through Labor Day. A few of these have a separate fee to access the boat ramp. For an additional fee, you can buy a permit from any state park office that allows unlimited access to most state parks. With the exception of Union Lake, only electric outboards are allowed on Wildlife Management Area waters in New Jersey.

While scouting for potential sites, I talked to people—park rangers, paddlers, local police officers, anglers, guides, and anyone I thought might know what was going on in the area. The outcome was information on two sites scheduled to open for public access in the summer of 2001: Splitrock Reservoir in Morris County and Whites Pond in Sussex County. I also found one site that had just recently opened up, Paulins Kill Lake in Sussex County. I learned that one site previously accessible was now closed, preventing me from making a long trip for nothing or, worse yet, confronting an irate landowner.

This book can never be complete. Lands around lakes and ponds are bought and sold continually, voiding or allowing public access. New housing developments and roads that spring up may render a site much less desirable or accessible. Contacts made during the compilation of this book will help keep me posted on changes in specific areas. With your help, future editions will include additional paddling sites and updated information on current ones. Your opinions and thoughts about these sites are important. Perhaps you know of a good lake I missed, notice some inaccuracy in this edition, or discover changes to existing sites. If so, please pass them along to me: Kathy Kenley, c/o AMC Books, 5 Joy Street, Boston, MA 02108. Enjoy the adventure—now, get out and paddle!

Map Legend

————— major highway

———— state highway

——— paved road

::::::::::: dirt road

------------ foot path

+++++++ railroad tracks

〜〜 stream

▬ ▬ ▬ ▬ dike

P parking

⌣ launch

⸜⸝ marsh

⌂ tents

◢ lean-tos

🏠 cabins

🪑 picnic area

🛝 playground

☼ hills

▢ old foundations/ruins

■ park headquarters/visitor's center

Trip Locator and Map

Trip Highlights Chart

Location	No.	Trip	Page No.	Level of Difficulty*
Northern New Jersey	1	Steeny Kill and Sawmill Lakes	2	easy
	2	Lake Aeroflex, Gardner's Pond, Twin Lakes, and Whites Pond	6	easy
	3	Hackensack Meadows	11	moderate
	4	Pompton Lake	15	easy
	5	Shepherd Lake	18	moderate
	6	Monksville Reservoir	21	moderate/difficult
	7	Green Turtle Lake	24	easy/moderate
	8	Wawayanda Lake	27	moderate
	9	Swartswood and Paulins Kill Lakes	32	easy/moderate
	10	White's Lake	37	easy
	11	Oxford Furnace Lake	40	easy
	12	Columbia Lake	42	easy
	13	Merrill Creek Reservoir	44	moderate/difficult
	14	Lakes Hopatcong and Musconectcong	47	moderate/difficult
	15	Silver Lake	53	easy
	16	Cranberry Lake	56	easy/moderate
	17	Splitrock Reservoir	61	moderate/difficult

Easy: shallow and more protected; ideal for novice paddlers and families with small children

Moderate: a potentially strong current or large, open body of water subject to high winds; a degree of caution should be observed

Difficult: a large, deep body of water, or a body of water subject to high winds and/or boat traffic; caution should be observed

Camping	Hiking	Picnic Area	Playground	Outboards Permitted	Boat Ramp
✔	✔	✔		✔	
✔	✔	✔		✔	✔
		✔	✔	✔	✔
		✔		✔	✔
	✔	✔	✔	✔	✔
				✔	✔
	✔			✔	
✔	✔	✔	✔	✔	✔
✔	✔	✔	✔	✔	✔
✔				✔	
✔	✔	✔	✔	✔	✔
✔	✔				
	✔	✔		✔	✔
✔		✔	✔	✔	✔
✔				✔	
	✔			✔	✔
	✔			unknown	

Easy: shallow and more protected; ideal for novice paddlers and families with small children

Moderate: a potentially strong current or large, open body of water subject to high winds; a degree of caution should be observed

Difficult: a large, deep body of water, or a body of water subject to high winds and/or boat traffic; caution should be observed

Camping	Hiking	Picnic Area	Playground	Outboards Permitted	Boat Ramp
	✔	✔			
	✔	✔			
	✔	✔	✔		✔
	✔	✔	✔	✔	✔
	✔			✔	✔
				✔	✔
	✔	✔			
✔	✔	✔	✔	✔	✔
✔	✔	✔	✔	✔	✔
	✔	✔	✔	✔	✔
	✔	✔			✔
	✔	✔		✔	
	✔			✔	
	✔			✔	
	✔	✔	✔		✔

Easy: shallow and more protected; ideal for novice paddlers and families with small children

Moderate: a potentially strong current or large, open body of water subject to high winds; a degree of caution should be observed

Difficult: a large, deep body of water, or a body of water subject to high winds and/or boat traffic; caution should be observed

Camping	Hiking	Picnic Area	Playground	Outboards Permitted	Boat Ramp
✔	✔			✔	
✔	✔	✔	✔	✔	✔
				✔	✔
✔	✔			✔	
	✔	✔	N/Y	✔	N/Y
	✔			✔	
	✔				
✔	✔	✔	N/Y	✔	✔
✔				✔	✔
	✔	✔		✔	✔
✔	✔	✔		✔	
	✔	✔		✔	
	✔	✔	✔	✔	✔
✔	✔	✔	✔	✔	✔
✔	✔	✔	✔	✔	
✔	✔			✔	
	✔	✔			
✔	✔	✔	✔	✔	

Northern New Jersey

Northwest New Jersey includes most of the state's largest natural lakes and natural or human-made reservoirs tucked in valleys between the mountains that comprise part of the Appalachian Ridge and Valley Region and the Piedmont Plateau. Creeks and streams along the western edge of the state drain into the Delaware River. From the central and eastern portions of the state, they drain into the Hudson River or the Atlantic Ocean.

The Appalachian Trail traverses the crest of the Kittatinney Ridge in the northwest corner of the state, where black bears, coyotes, and bobcat are seen frequently. Limestone, shale, siltstone, sandstone, and gneiss compose most of the rock types here along with smaller amounts of quartzite and schist. Volcanic activity during continental rifting left behind the durable basalt of the Watchung and Orange Mountains and the Palisades Sill. Geologically recent ice ages carved out numerous glacial lakes, such as Hopatcong and Swartswood, which are now fed by winter snowmelts and natural runoff. Glaciers once deeply gouged the valley now occupied by Lake Aeroflex.

Population density on New Jersey's eastern side, across the Hudson River from New York City, is the highest in the state. Cities such as Newark, Jersey City, and Patterson meld together as one and extend their urban sprawl farther west each year. Conservation of undisturbed lands in and around this vicinity is most critical for wildlife habitat preservation.

Steeny Kill and Sawmill Lakes
High Point (Sussex)

On the drive along Route 23 to High Point State Park in the extreme northwest corner of the state, be prepared for some steep hills in this mountainous region within the Appalachian Ridge and Valley Region. As you can guess by the park's name, you will find in its boundaries the highest elevation in the state, which is marked by a 220-foot monument. High Point Mountain rises 1,804 feet above sea level—not much by "real" mountain standards, but it's ours. High Point Mountain is part of the Appalachian Trail, a continuous footpath that starts at Springer Mountain in Georgia, and passes through this park on the way to its northern terminus at Katahdin in Maine—a distance of more than 2,000 miles!

At the visitor center pick up maps and pamphlets that show hiking trails, campgrounds, roads to the two lakes, and directions to the High Point monument. Gas engines are prohibited at both lakes, and the only swimming beach is on Lake Marcia, which is not open to boating. More than 15 miles of mixed-use trails weave through the park, some of them possessing moderately steep sections over rocky terrain.

Black bears, bobcat, deer, and fox are among the wildlife found inside the park's hardwood and conifer forests. At 30 acres, Steeny Kill Lake is the larger of the two lakes. Hickory, beech, and red maple prevail in the more open areas on the south shore. I personally prefer Steeny Kill Lake for kayaking; not because it's larger, but because it has an irregular shoreline with more nooks and crannies to explore. If you enjoy birding, keep alert for Cooper's and red-shouldered hawks. Bog and wood turtles inhabit the swampy southern end of the lake.

Sawmill Lake lies at the bottom of a depression on the south side of High Point Mountain. The 20-acre lake is roughly elliptical, with a

Lake
Marcia
(no boating)

High
Point
Mountain

Steeny Kill
Lake

Route 23

To
Colesville

Sawmill Road

N

0   1/4   1/2
mile

Sawmill
Lake

few coves on the eastern and southern shores. Tall pine, oak, and hickory dominate the woods around the lake, and rustic tent sites and a few cabins sit along the eastern lakeshore. It was here that I ended my day. Before retiring, I paddled out to the middle of the lake, sat under a quarter moon, and watched the stars while frogs called to each other in the night. It was August, and the Perseid meteor showers graced me with two shooting starts—the end of a perfect day.

Getting there

Drive north on Route 23 out of Colesville for about 2.4 miles to the park office located on the left side of the road. Proceed another 0.5 mile past the park office to Sawmill Lake; turn left and follow the main road 1.8 miles to the lake. The launch site and parking areas are designated.

Steeny Kill Lake in High Point State Park is one of the highest-elevation lakes in the state.

A view of campsites along the eastern shore of Sawmill Lake.

The Steeny Kill Lake entrance is 1.6 miles north of the park office on the right-hand side of Route 23 (1.1 miles north of the entrance to Sawmill Lake). It's only a short drive off the road to the launch site and parking area.

A small fee is charged in summer at the park's recreational site across the road from the visitor center, but access to both lakes is free. Wildlife, artifact, and geological exhibits in the center are worth a visit. High Point State Park, 1480 State Route 23, Sussex, NJ 07461-3605; 973-875-4800.

Lake Aeroflex, Gardner's Pond, Twin Lakes, and Whites Pond
Newton (Sussex)

Four bodies of water reside within Kittatinny Valley State Park, and at 110 feet, Lake Aeroflex is reportedly the deepest natural glacial lake in the state. Situated just outside the mountainous Appalachian Ridge and Valley Region, the land here starts giving way to the gentle rolling hills of the Piedmont Plateau.

Large horse and agricultural farms become more frequent as you drive through the countryside. Aeroflex-Andover airport sits between Lake Aeroflex and Gardner's Pond. Normally I would stay away from airports, but this is a small local airport with infrequent activity. Somehow the small planes taking off or landing lend an air of adventure to the setting. No air traffic can be heard from Twin Lakes or Whites Pond, located on the other side of the park.

Lake Aeroflex stretches its long and narrow 117 acres parallel to Limecrest Road (Route 669) on the northwest side of the quiet town of Andover. Ducks and geese are abundant on the shallower western shores, where clumps of aquatic grasses provide ideal foraging. Bog and painted turtles frequently sun themselves along the banks, and snapping turtles hide in the sediment on the lake bottom. Trees along the eastern shore between the lake and Limecrest Road afford visual and auditory screening from the sparse road traffic. About eight picnic tables are scattered under large trees in the open area adjacent to the park office and launching ramp. No one was on the lake when I paddled it, although local construction workers used the picnic area during their lunch break and a young mother took her two children for a brief stroll around the grounds. Swimming and motors are not permitted on any waters within the park, and only Lake Aeroflex has picnic facilities.

Gardner's Pond is located at the southern end of the airport. Only airport vehicular traffic is allowed along the road, but you can carry your boat or use a portable wheeled-cart to travel 0.5 mile to the launch. It was dusk by the time I finished kayaking Lake Aeroflex and Twin Lakes, preventing further investigation. A local fisherman came from the pond and remarked, "The fishin's good, but the pond is kinda small." Perhaps next time I'll explore it.

Twin Lakes provides quaint paddling waters, where a couple of local swans may accompany you. Two bodies of water connected by a

At 110 feet, Lake Aeroflex is the deepest natural glacial lake in New Jersey.

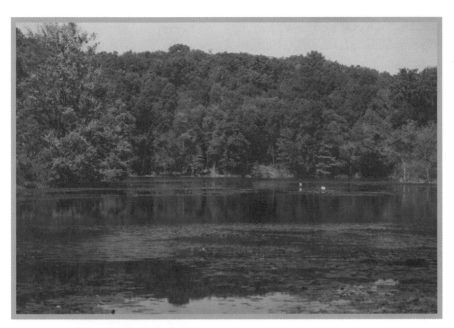

Two swans accompany me for part of my paddle. Narrow passages on the right and left lead to separate lakes.

narrow neck not far from the launch site give this lake an hourglass shape. About 0.25 mile from the launch, you can choose to go right or left. The right side leads you to waters where short hills rise steeply from the shore. This is a great place to watch for belted kingfishers that build nests in cavities along the steep embankments a few feet above the water's surface. I spotted three in the short time I paddled that section, along with numerous frogs and spotted turtles. The brightly colored northern red salamander hides under logs on shore.

Whites Pond and the surrounding land, which has been purchased recently with Green Acre funds, will be open to the public by summer 2001. I noticed that beaver activity on its far side had rerouted the water flow, making most of the pond too shallow to paddle. One ranger mentioned that when the pond is prepared for public use, the beaver dams might be removed to increase water flow and depth.

Camping is available at Columbia Valley Campground, 3 Ghost Pony Road, Andover, N J 07821; 973-691-0596.

Getting there

To Lake Aeroflex and Gardner's Pond: Take Exit 25 off I-80; drive north about 7.0 miles on Route 206 to Andover, where Routes 517 and 613 intersect. Continue north 0.7 mile on Route 206 to Route 669 (Limecrest Road); turn right onto Limecrest Road and drive 1.1 miles to the Kittatinny Valley State Park entrance on the left. The visitor center, boat ramp, parking, and picnic tables are within 200 feet of the entrance.

To Twin Lakes and Whites Pond: From Route 669, drive north 0.9 mile on Route 206, turn right onto Goodale Road, and drive 0.6 mile to the fenced entrance on the left. Drive across the parking area to the short gravel road leading to the launch site. On your way to Twin Lakes you will pass Whites Pond, open to the public in 2001, on your right about halfway up Goodale Road. Kittatinny Valley State Park, P.O. Box 621, Andover, N J 07821-0521; 973-786-6445.

Hackensack Meadows
Secaucus (Hudson)

You're probably thinking, "Secaucus? This is supposed to be a book on good, quiet paddling sites!" I'm sure you think it crazy to suggest paddling anywhere in this highly industrialized, overly populated area. For those living nearby, Hackensack Meadows offers one of the few spots to paddle within a reasonable distance. It also helps us realize how important it is to protect such precious environments for wildlife and public enjoyment in the midst of highly developed cities. I also admit the desire to find at least one decent paddling location in every county, even tiny Hudson County.

The Hackensack Riverkeeper Canoe Project's main goal is to have Hackensack Meadows designated as a National Wildlife Reserve to protect it from further development. The organization maintains a base of operation in a small trailer next to the boat ramp, where they rent canoes, run eco-cruises, organize river cleanups, and distribute literature to foster public awareness of this valuable environment.

Migrating birds use the meadows to rest and feed before continuing their journeys. Some stay to grace the state with their presence throughout the warmer months, and a few become year-round residents in this rich estuarine environment where the Hackensack River winds through the marshes. Birds frequently seen here include egrets, herons, yellowlegs, stilt and semipalmated sandpipers, least and Forster's terns, and black skimmer. Watch the terns as they hunt for prey, hover in place 20 to 40 feet above the water, then plunge straight down for the catch. Scan the mudflats carefully for the occasional avocet, and the grassy shallows for common moorhen. Look carefully at the edges of marsh grass for yellow- and black-crowned night herons, a delightful find. Paddle up and down the river and inspect side channels where feeder streams enter, as wading birds are often found there.

The Hackensack River is a few hundred yards wide here and, with nothing but open salt marshes all around, can churn up pretty well on a windy day. Keep alert to changes in weather and observe the same caution here as you would on a large lake. From the boat launch, the best paddling is to your right (upriver), where numerous feeder streams and small creeks offer hours of exploration. Look carefully at the grassy corners for the gnawed, telltale sign of muskrat activity, then see if you can find their mounded house about 15 feet or so back from the water.

The diamondback terrapin, *Malaclemys terrapin*, is the only turtle in the continental United States that is found solely in brackish saltwater environments. Aside from habitat, concentric rings or ridges on its shell, and a spotted head and limbs confirm this reptile's identification. Females can attain a length of 9 inches, but males reach only 5.5 inches. I haven't heard of many sightings here, since they are highly susceptible to pollution—another good reason to support efforts to have this site designated a National Wildlife Reserve. For further

Great egrets search for food in the shallow waters of a channel leading off the Hackensack River.

information, contact Hackensack Riverkeeper Inc. in residence at Fairleigh Dickinson University, 1000 River Road–T090C, Teaneck, NJ 07666; 201-692-8440.

If you go left (downstream) from the ramp, do not go past the third bridge (ignore railroad bridges) about 3.0 miles down. It becomes heavily industrialized, and you'll be within 4.0 miles of Newark Bay, where tidal currents strengthen.

Getting there

Unless you're used to congested traffic, the first thing you'll want to do is have directions written out, large and legible, and by your side. There is rarely a place to pull over and refer to a book; traffic is moving at a chaotic pace.

From east of Newark, take Route 78 east and get off at Exit 58B onto Pulaski Skyway (Routes 1–9) north. Look for signs for "last exit before toll." Stay in the left-hand lane, following signs for Tonnele Avenue. Exit at the Tonnele/Lincoln Tunnel—stay to the right coming off the exit. At the bottom of the ramp, you will be at a circle. Stay right around the circle (about a quarter of the way around), following signs for Routes 1–9 north (Tonnele Avenue). Look for Manhattan Street 0.6 mile down Tonnele Avenue, and get in the right-hand lane to take the jug-handle onto County Road, 0.1 mile past Manhattan (you will have to make a left-hand turn from the right-hand lane). OK, you can breathe now, you're almost there.

Follow County Road to the T, about 2.5 miles, and turn left onto New County Road. A few blocks down, the road will bend to the right. Look for the sign "Hudson County Park at Laurel Hill" on your left about 200 feet past the bend; turn left into the park and follow signs to the boat launch on the right. You made it!

Pompton Lake
Pompton Lakes (Passaic)

The majority of lakeside property on Pompton Lake is privately owned, but most of the houses are on large properties set back from the shoreline and screened by trees, providing pleasant paddling conditions. Willow scattered along the shore drape long, delicate branches that shimmer with the slightest breeze. Ducks, geese, and swans forage among vegetation in shallow waters of this long, 204-acre lake. Paddle to the northern end of the lake from the put-in to circle a small island on the west side immediately past the bridge at Lakeside Avenue.

A duck floats on the waters of Pompton Lake.

Terhune Drive

Route 202

To
Route 287

Basswood

Pompton
Lake

Route 202

P

Lamoureaux Lane

N

0   1/4   1/2
mile

Patterson–Hamburg Turnpike

Route 202

Pompton Lake can be accessed from the public boat launch in Terhune Memorial Park on the eastern side of the lake. For a lunch break, stop at the picnic tables or the small pagoda situated close to the water's edge under the huge park trees. While motorboats are permitted on the lake, a ten-horsepower limit is imposed. Swimming is not allowed.

Getting there

From the south, take Route 202 north into the town of Pompton Lakes, where it becomes part of the Patterson-Hamburg Turnpike. Route 202 turns right in the center of town onto Terhune Drive; continue north 0.9 mile on Route 202 (Terhune Drive). The park entrance will be on your left, 50 feet past Lamoureaux Lane, which will be on your right. The entrance to the park is tricky, as signs are not visible until you are almost at the narrow entrance road flanked by large stone pillars. The boat ramp is on the right side of the parking area. If the ramp gate is closed, you can carry your boat from the parking lot to the water, a distance of about 100 feet.

From the north, take Route 287 to Exit 58 and drive south on Route 202 about 2.9 miles to Lakeside Avenue, which crosses over the lake on your right. Drive 0.3 mile past Lakeside Avenue to the park entrance on your right. New Jersey Division of Fish and Wildlife, Northern Region Office, 26 Route 173 West, Hampton, NJ 08827; 973-383-0918.

Shepherd Lake
Ringwood (Passaic)

Tucked snuggly in the northeast corner of Ringwood State Park along the New York border, the 74-acre Shepherd Lake is completely enclosed by hills densely packed with stately pine, hemlock, and various hardwoods. Pink mountain laurel brighten the woods during early summer, and large maple and poplar jutting out between dense evergreens create a magnificent palette of fall colors. As you drive the mountainous road to the lake, look for large boulders, called erratics, that dot the landscape: remnants of the last Ice Age.

Around the shoreline toward the east end of the lake you will quickly lose sight of the bathing beach and enjoy exploring big coves and little inlets framed by hemlock, pine, and maple. Gulls visiting the lake dive for fish in the clear, spring-fed waters, and blue jays screech their way through the surrounding forest. On open lakes like this, keep your eyes peeled for soaring eagles and hawks. Fishing is excellent throughout the lake; trout, pickerel, and largemouth bass are the primary catch of most anglers. These spring-fed mountain waters remain quite brisk throughout the summer, so be wary of hypothermia, and always take adequate clothing along even on the hottest days.

Miles of hiking trails surround the lake and meander through the park. Contact the New York/New Jersey Trail Conference at 212-685-9699 for a trail map of the park. If you desire to venture out on a long hike, make sure you have a map, compass, water, and snacks. Let someone know that you are hiking, and your intended route.

Only electric outboards are permitted on the lake. Picnic tables, a basketball court, food concessions, and a small playground surround the open recreation area next to the swimming beach on the southwest corner of the lake. A small entrance fee is charged between Memorial Day and Labor Day to cover the cost of seasonal help, but off-season access is free. Sadly, there is no camping available inside the park.

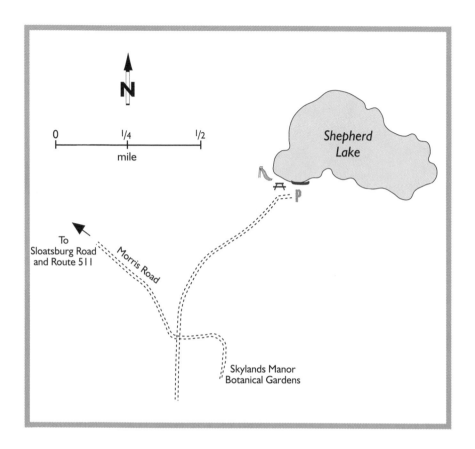

Ringwood State Park and its surrounding lands once housed important iron-producing complexes during the industry's heyday in the eighteenth and nineteenth centuries. From the mid-1700s, the Ringwood Company's iron forges and furnaces supplied the colonies with products for more than a hundred years and contributed to war efforts during the American Revolution, the War of 1812, and the Civil War. Ringwood Manor, a 41-room mansion located inside the park, was home to the local ironmasters.

If you have time, I recommend stopping at the unique Botanical Gardens at Skylands Manor. You will pass a sign pointing to the garden on the way to Shepherd Lake. A Tudor-style manor house at the entrance serves as an information center and the hub for local horticultural clubs. Marked serpentine roads meander through 96 acres

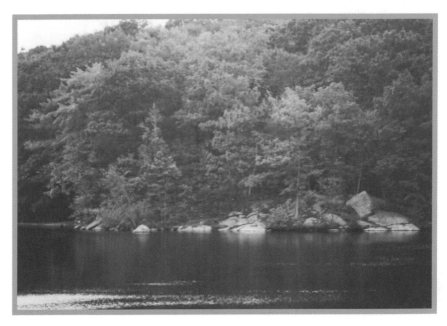
Rocky shorelines and hemlock are typical of mountain lakes.

of natural and formal wildflower gardens, trees, shrubs, and bogs. Most of the roads are one-way, encouraging a leisurely drive, but biking or walking are the best ways to enjoy these magnificent gardens.

Getting there

From the south, take Exit 55 off I-287, drive north 7.3 miles on Route 511 (Ringwood Avenue), and turn right onto Sloatsburg Road. Beautiful Wanaque Reservoir will be on your left—no boating is allowed on the reservoir. Drive 2.3 miles on Sloatsburg Road, turn right onto Morris Road, and drive 1.4 miles. At the intersection a sign directs you to Shepherd Lake on the left, about 1.0 mile down the road. Signs also point straight ahead to the botanical gardens less than 0.25 mile away. Stay to the right after the tollbooth for the boat ramp and parking area. Ringwood State Park, 1304 Sloatsburg Road, Ringwood, NJ 07456; 973-962-7031.

Monksville Reservoir
West Milford (Passaic)

Want a nice long paddle and some great fishing? Then visit the 505-acre Monksville Reservoir that encircles Long Pond Ironworks State Park like a giant horseshoe. You'll find the most interesting paddling on the far side of the reservoir, where coves of all sizes form a continuous string along the highly irregular shoreline. White birches seem particularly abundant around the lake, contrasting sharply against dark evergreens. Ducks and geese can be found around the lake in the protected coves. Of all the fish that inhabit these waters, big muskellunge is the most sought after by anglers. Prehistoric-looking snapping turtles inhabit the lake, but are seen rarely as they spend most of their time underwater (unlike other turtles, which like to bask in the sun).

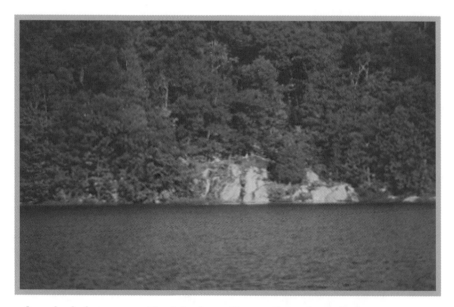

A rocky ledge across the lake from the northern launch site.

The northern end of the reservoir passes under the bridge at Route 511 and the scenery changes to a more shallow, marshlike environment. That's what I like about paddling under bridges; I just might be surprised by something different on the other side. To the left, a large field of drowned trees sticks out of shallow waters, inviting you to weave in and out looking for turtles sunning themselves on low stumps. Dense clumps of aquatic grasses create perfect nursery grounds for large lake fish. Bird watching here is also quite different, as warblers and finches visibly flit about and pileated woodpeckers nest in cavities of dead trees. To the right, a small boat shed on a wooden dock rents canoes. Open grassy areas invite you to pull up, stop for lunch, and stretch your legs.

Long Pond Iron Works historical site, located just north of the reservoir on Route 511, offers visitors the opportunity to tour the ruins of three furnaces and buildings of the old iron-smelting complex. Peter Hasenclever founded the operation in 1766. It was run by a succession of famous ironmasters, including Robert Erskin and Abram Hewitt, for almost 200 years. The park is listed on the State and National Registers of Historic Places.

Getting there

There are two boat ramps on the reservoir. From the south, take Exit 55 off I-287 and drive north on Route 511 (Ringwood Avenue) about 7.0 miles to Sloatsburg Road on your right. Continue on Route 511 another 1.3 miles to Stonetown Road on your left. The first gated entrance is on the left 0.3 mile north of Stonetown Road. A second gated entrance, again on your left, can be found at the other end of the reservoir, 0.7 mile north on Route 511 past the first gate.

Both launch sites have well-maintained portable toilets. A ten-horsepower limit is imposed on all motorboats, but weekends during prime fishing season may be a little noisy in the early morning hours when most anglers head for their favorite spots. Swimming is not permitted. Long Pond Ironworks State Park, Route 511, Greenwood Lake Turnpike, Ringwood, NJ; 201-962-7031.

Green Turtle Lake
West Milford (Passaic)

Don't miss this gem! Driving down the steep potholed road to the lake for the first time, I came around the last bend and stepped on the brakes. Islands, two of them, jutted out of the water a couple hundred yards offshore from the dirt and stone ramp ahead; I couldn't wait to get my kayak into the water. Islands not only provide more shoreline to explore, but they visually break up the lake's surface, creating a feeling of adventure. At the sound of my car creeping toward the ramp, a female mallard, ten feet away, quickly escorted her brood toward dense shrubs farther along the edge; I had disturbed their tranquil swim.

Tucked in a valley with steep mountains on three sides, this is a great place to come on windy days. On either side of the ramp, cedar and red maple can be seen among aquatic plants and grasses. Turkey vultures soar on warm thermals of air along the steep mountainside on the northern edge of the lake. Only one other boat was on the lake that first day, an electric outboard with two anglers. We nodded in recognition, but exchanged no words.

Several narrow animal paths lead to the lake and you can usually spot a number of deer. Two dead trees on the larger island showed evidence of recent woodpecker activity, as the wood was not weathered-looking; perhaps one had nested there earlier that summer. The rocky outcroppings on the island's north end may harbor timber rattlesnakes or northern copperheads, both of which are poisonous. Exercise caution if you climb the hills.

Camping around the lake is the only thing missing here. Located inside Wanaque Wildlife Management Area, only electric outboards are permitted on the lake. No formal swimming beach, picnic tables, or facilities of any kind—just a dirt and stone ramp leading to a pristine environment. Go for it!

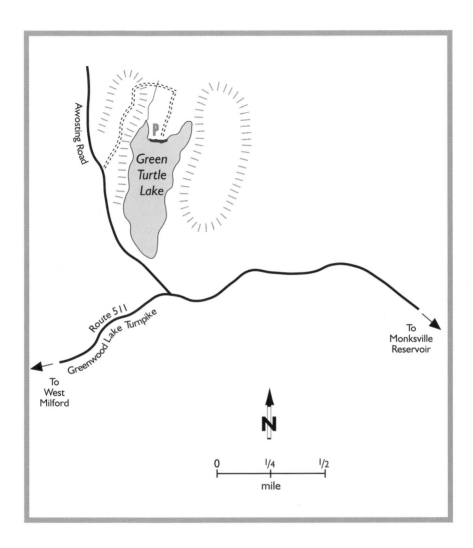

Getting there

Starting on Greenwood Lake Turnpike in West Milford, drive south 0.8 mile on Route 511, then turn left onto Awosting Road. Be careful here as this is a hairpin turn. Drive 0.6 mile on Awosting Road to the Wildlife Management Area entrance. A large sign is at the entrance, but it sits back from the road partially hidden by trees. The best bet is to look for two stone pillars, one on each side of the road, about 500 feet before the

Two islands to explore a few hundred yards south of the launch site.

entrance. Each pillar is approximately three feet square and five feet high. Once partially blacktopped, the steep road leading down to the lake is now extremely potholed. The road widens near the lake, providing ample parking. North Jersey District Water Supply Commission, One F. A. Orechio Drive, Wanaque, NJ 07465; 973-836-3600.

Wawayanda Lake
Vernon (Sussex)

Nestled within the vast mountains of Wawayanda State Park, this large mountain lake will provide days of enjoyable paddling. Camping is available, but I would advise making reservations if you intend to visit during the summer. Picnic grounds, a sandy bathing beach, a playground, and boat rentals all are situated at the large recreational area on the north side of the lake. Weekends in July and August can be extremely crowded with hikers, anglers, and vacationers.

I camped here in August for two weekdays, but cool winds were blowing a little more than 12 MPH both days, possibly keeping many from engaging in beach activities or paddling. Later in the day, winds gusting to 16 MPH over the large, 255-acre lake created small whitecaps. Several deep coves and half a dozen islands provide a welcome shelter from vigorous paddling conditions on windy days. Duck into a cove or around to the lee side of an island for a rest, if you encounter adverse conditions.

Other than self-propelled boats, only quiet electric outboards are permitted. You can escape the more populated recreation areas next to the launch site by paddling toward the southern end of this long lake. Distance and tree-covered islands will soon block most audible sounds of civilization. Though a multitude of canoes are available for rent, most people do not venture past the middle of the lake, making the southern end more peaceful.

Wawayanda Lake is a good place to try your luck at fishing. Depths range from just a few feet close to shore to about 90 feet in the center of the northern half of the lake. Trout, largemouth bass, catfish, yellow perch, and large sunfish swim beneath the surface, any one of which would taste delicious cooked over a campfire at day's end. One fish with a long history on earth, the bowfin, also can be found in the lake.

Warwick

Double Pond Road

Route 513

Clinton Road

To Route 23

Scott Island

Wawayanda Lake

Rock Island

Beech Island

N

0   1/4   1/2

mile

The wind finally dies off near the end of the day, as the sun dips behind one of the islands.

Look closely in the long, shallow inlets and you might be lucky enough to see a river otter.

Hiking and biking trails meander for more than 40 miles throughout 12,000 acres of Atlantic white cedar swamps and hardwood forests. Wood and bog turtles inhabit swampy areas along with raccoons, possum, and skunk. A 20-mile stretch of the Appalachian Trail runs along the western boundary, crossing deep ravines and climbing to sensational mountaintop views. Watch out for rattlesnakes and copperheads when hiking the trails, as they often warm themselves on sunny rocks or ground. Throughout the park, bird life is bountiful. Red-shouldered hawk, great blue heron, vultures, eagles, warblers, orioles, and various songbirds are there if you are observant.

Start out early in the morning for the most peaceful paddling. That's also the best time to check out the bird populations and look for other wildlife such as raccoons, coyotes, gray fox, and deer, as they are most active just after dawn.

Bear-crossing signs posted on many roads should help you remember to be careful about food while camping. Seal all containers tightly, and put them in your car when you're finished eating. An excellent pamphlet on do's and don'ts while in bear country is available at the visitor center. Get it. Read it.

Getting there

Drive south 0.2 mile on Route 23 from Route 171 to the Clinton Road exit. Drive north on Clinton Road about 7.0 miles until you come to the T-junction at Route 513 (Warwick Turnpike). Turn left (north) onto Route 513 and drive 2.3 miles to the park entrance on your left. Stop at the visitor center to pick up a map and other useful pamphlets. From the visitor center, continue 1.9 miles to the turnoff for the recreation area. The road to the boat launch will be on your left. The park is open from 6:00 A.M. to 8:00 P.M. Wawayanda State Park, 885 Warwick Turnpike, Hewitt, NJ 07421; 973-853-4468.

Bowfin
(Amia calva)

The only extant representative of the family *Amiidae*, bowfin date back to the early-Jurassic period about 100 million years ago when dinosaurs roamed the earth. A bony gular plate located between the jaws on its underside is a distinctive characteristic of this olive-colored fish with a long, low dorsal fin and a partially lobed caudal fin (tail). Males have a black spot ringed with yellow or orange at the upper base of the tail; females have a similar spot but no ring. Hard plates in the mouth wreak havoc on anglers' hooks, and their sharp teeth can cut through line—and fingers—readily. Like gar, bowfin have a modified air bladder that enables them to breathe surface air and thus tolerate stagnant, oxygen-depleted waters.

Although the majority of the extinct bowfin forms were marine, the modern bowfin is restricted to the sluggish-moving streams and backwaters of eastern North America, the same environment as bass and crappie. Voracious feeders, bowfin have been known to decimate local game-fish populations on occasion. Their primary diet consists of crustaceans, insects, larvae, and small fish. Adults attain lengths of 18 to 42 inches and can reach weights up to 20 pounds. While considered poor eating, they are sought by anglers for the feisty fight they provide. Use the same bait and tackle to catch them as you would for bass.

Bowfin breed in spring after an elaborate ritual during which they construct bowl-shaped nests by tearing out weeds in a shallow area. Once a female is attracted to the nest, spawning commences. Males guard the eggs and fry for several weeks and may mate with several females during that time, thus having eggs in various stages of development. Young are equipped with an adhesive organ on their snout that enables them to hold on to weeds and remain at the nest site. Their rapid growth rate allows them to reach lengths up to nine inches in their first year.

Swartswood and Paulins Kill Lakes
Swartswood (Sussex)

Swartswood and Paulins Kill Lakes in the northwest mountains of the state can be accessed through Swartswood State Park, which offers camping, picnicking, playgrounds, and swimming. Neither lake lies completely within the park's boundary, so you will find private property at various points on the south and west sides. For the most part, the houses are set back from the tree-lined shores and do not detract from the setting.

Stop at the park office on Route 619 for a map and information about camping. Tent/trailer campsites and three yurts (circular tents built on a wood frame featuring a deck and a Plexiglas skylight) are available. Swartswood Lake gives you 500 acres in which to paddle. Hours can be spent exploring the numerous coves and peninsulas along the perimeter. According to locals, fishing is good in both lakes, with walleye and brown trout the best catches. Mountain laurel and mulberry bushes grow in the shade of pine, oak, ash, birch, and hickory trees. Birding is excellent, with a number of observation facilities within the park: watch carefully and you might catch a glimpse of the colorful scarlet tanager. Butterflies, essential to the pollination process of many botanical species, dance from wildflower to wildflower along the sunny shores. Since the swimming beach is located at the extreme northern end, it is quite easy to escape into quieter waters by paddling south (left) from the launch. Hiking and nature trails lead through upland forests and bogs within the 1,357-acre park. A small car-top launch area is also available on the southern end of Swartswood Lake.

Paulins Kill Lake is unique due to its extremely long and narrow shape. A private community gobbles up the land on the southern half of the lake. Most of the homes sit back from the shoreline, but their docks

N

0   1/4   1/2
mile

Parsons Road

Junction Road

P

Paulins Kill
Lake

Route 521/West Shore Drive

Little
Swartswood
Lake

Route 622

P

Swartswood
Lake

Route 619

P

Route 521/West Shore Drive

P

Route 614

To
Fredon
and Route 94

are prominent features. Only a few private properties adjoin the lake in the northern section above the Route 622 bridge where the New Jersey Division of Fish and Wildlife recently acquired a large parcel of land through the Green Acres Program. There are no recreational facilities here—just a boat ramp for a quiet paddle on the northern end. Dense stands of hemlock within mixed-hardwood forests on the east hillsides are breathtaking, and the steep banks provide perfect habitat for kingfisher. A few small low-lying dirt edges allow you to stop for a lunch break or stretch your legs. I thoroughly enjoyed paddling this lake, particularly the upper portion on state-owned property. This would be a

Arrow weed cluster near a shallow bank at the southern end of Swartswood Lake.

Looking down a small section of the three-mile-long lake.

great location on windier days when you want to get a good workout, as its narrow width offers protection from all but the windiest conditions.

Getting there

Access to Swartswood State Park is conveniently located near the junction of Routes 622 and 619 about 2.0 miles west of Route 94. From Route 619, drive west 0.5 mile on Route 622 to the entrance for Little Swartswood Lake boat launch. To access Swartswood Lake from the same junction, drive south 1.0 mile on Route 619 to the boat launch on your right. Maps can be picked up at the park office and visitor center located 0.6 mile south on Route 619. The swimming beach, playground, and picnic areas are also located there.

From Route 94 in the town of Fredon, drive west 2.3 miles on Route 614 (Paulins Kill Lake Road), turn right onto Route 619, and drive 1.8 miles to the main park entrance on your left.

A car-top launch is available at the extreme southern end of Swartswood Lake. From Route 622, drive south 2.3 miles on Route 521. You will see a very small boat launch sign on your left. The launch is 150 feet off the road with parking available for about eight cars. This is a pretty spot tucked in the woods and a great spot for an informal picnic before or after your paddle.

Access to nearby Paulins Kill Lake is only a ten-minute drive from the junction of Routes 622 and 619. From Route 619, drive east 1.9 miles on Route 622, turn left onto Junction Road for 1.0 mile, then left onto Parsons Road. Caution! Immediately after turning onto Parsons Road, you will go under a very narrow railroad trestle that is little more than one car width. Continue on Parsons Road 0.4 mile to the roadside parking area and boat launch on your left. The small dirt clearing with a few shrubs and saplings is easily overlooked. Swartswood State Park, P.O. Box 123, Swartswood, NJ 07887-0123; 973-383-5230.

White's Lake
Squires Corner (Warren)

White's Lake is totally enclosed by a Natural Reserve Area in the rural countryside of western Warren County. Vegetation in the narrow strip between the lake and the road consists of tall grasses and a few saplings. Thick stands of Phragmites reed on either side of the launch site provide ample screening from the road. Dense woods surround the rest of the oval-shaped lake with red maple and other water-loving trees more common along the shoreline.

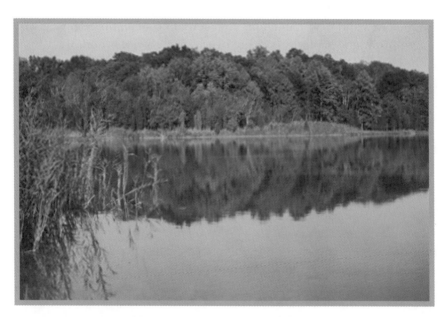

A stand of Phragmites provides seclusion from nearby rural road traffic. Hawks and wild turkeys are frequent visitors.

While not superbly scenic, White's Lake can provide a peaceful hour or two of paddling. The lake is surrounded by public property without recreational facilities. Wild carrot, butterfly-weed, thistle, goldenrod, and giant sunflower color grassy borders and attract butter-flies with their nectar. On the lake, painted and spotted turtles bask on fallen logs, while box turtles can be found under leaves in moist hollows on shore. Although I saw only turkey vultures, this should be a prime area to spot hawks that frequent nearby open fields in search of small rodents.

Camping is available at nearby Triplebrook Family Camping Resort on a 250-acre farm. Contact them at 58 Honey Run Road, Blairstown, NJ 07825; 888-343-CAMP.

Getting there

White's Lake Natural Reserve Area is located about 5.0 miles north of Blairstown along the east side of Route 521 (Stillwater Road), 0.4 mile north of the Route 659 junction. A few houses at that junction compose the blink-and-you'll-miss-it town of Squires Corner. A large reserve area sign is displayed prominently at the entrance to the gravel road leading to the lake and parking area visible from Route 521. New Jersey Division of Fish and Wildlife, Northern Region Office, 26 Route 173 West, Hampton, NJ 08827; 973-383-0918.

Oxford Furnace Lake
Oxford (Warren)

A furnace once operated in the small town of Oxford at the foot of the mountains during the heyday of the iron industry in the eighteenth and nineteenth centuries. The Green Acres Program contributed funds for the refurbishment of the 53-acre lake and surrounding property, with amenities including a soccer field, playground, picnic area, swimming

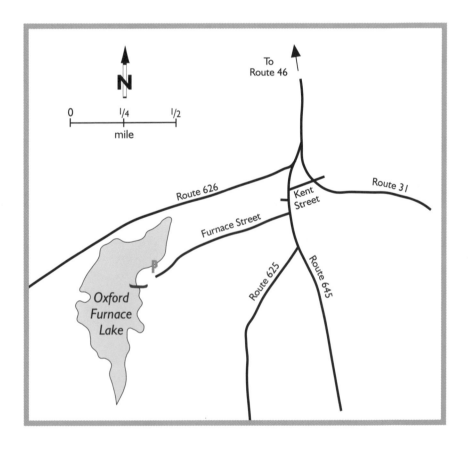

beach, and boat launch. It may be noisy on weekends, but with the lack of private property on the lake, you can escape the high-use recreation areas and enjoy the rest of the scenery. Wild grape leaves weave their tendrils around trees in open areas of the south end, inviting warblers, sparrows, and golden finches to nest. This would make an excellent alternative to Merrill Creek Reservoir (a half-hour drive south) on windy days.

Getting there

From Route 46, drive south on Route 31 about 2.0 miles to the town of Oxford. Look for Wall Street on your right and make the next right onto Kent Street. Drive two blocks to the T, turn left onto Route 625 for one block, then turn right onto Furnace Street. A billboard-sized sign for the newly renovated park is displayed proudly at the corner of Furnace Street and Route 625. For a small town, I found the streets a bit confusing—and changes were being made at one of the intersections. I know none of you want to do it, but, if all else fails, ask directions. New Jersey Division of Fish and Wildlife, Northern Region Office, 26 Route 173 West, Hampton, NJ 08827; 973-383-0918.

Columbia Lake
Polkville (Warren)

Long, narrow, and rather shallow, Columbia Lake is the place to go for bird watching. The only drawback is the proximity to noisy I-80, but visit the 40-acre lake anyway, especially if you enjoy birding. Its long, narrow islands and hammocks offer abundant shelter for waterfowl and provide an interesting trip as you weave in and out of the serpentine maze. Since much of the lake is shallow, frogs and turtles are plentiful, particularly in the northern half.

From the I-80 ramps, you get a magnificent view of the Delaware River Water Gap. Once a continuous east-west mountain ridge holding back a large inland sea, erosion worked on a weak spot, gradually

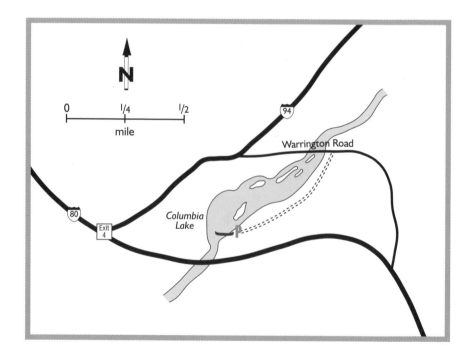

wearing it down until the waters started to escape. Once the outflow started, erosion accelerated, eventually creating a channel that would later become part of the Delaware River channel.

Camping is available at the heavily wooded Camp Taylor Campground, 85 Mount Pleasant Road, Columbia, NJ 07832; 908-496-4333. Miles of hiking trails connect to the Appalachian Trail system.

Getting there

Take I-80 to Exit 4, drive north 0.25 mile on Route 94, turn left, and drive 0.3 mile on Warrington Road. After crossing over a small bridge where Paulins Kill Creek flows into the lake, turn right onto the dirt road, and drive about 0.6 mile to the end. Because the dirt road parallels private property, it may appear to be part of a driveway. It isn't—that will become evident once you're past the house. A wooden sign for Columbia Lake is at the entrance, but it is dark with age and the lettering is barely visible when I visited. I suspect one good winter storm may knock it down. New Jersey Division of Fish and Wildlife, Northern Region Office, 26 Route 173 West, Hampton, NJ 08827; 973-383-0918.

Merrill Creek Reservoir
Stewartsville (Warren)

I found Merrill Creek Reservoir to be the least scenic (but still very nice) of the three large reservoirs in the area, which include Spruce Run and Round Valley, but at 650 acres it provides for a full day of exploration. Long stretches of dead trees rimming the shoreline near the launch did not make an appealing first impression, but once you're away from that area the scenery improves. There's no fee, even in summer, but there is a minimum length requirement for kayaks and canoes, 9 feet and 12 feet respectively.

Most of the shoreline is smooth, but if you paddle left from the launch site, a few large coves will spice up your paddling adventures. Water depth extends to 200 feet, so if you fish, make sure you have plenty of line on the reel. Largemouth and smallmouth bass, and brown and rainbow trout are the primary species preferred by anglers. Lights on two towers flash when winds exceed 25 MPH for five seconds or more, and all boats must head back to the launch. Sitting atop a mountain where vigorous winds can prevail, the warning lights provide an excellent safety measure. More than 2,000 acres of forested hills and mountains supply hikers and birders with miles of trails, one of which leads out from the northeast corner of the parking lot to a crest overlooking the reservoir. Maps can be picked up at the visitor center near the entrance. Swimming and camping are not permitted within the preserve.

Getting there

Take Exit 3 from I-78, following signs for Route 22. Drive west 0.6 mile on Route 22 and exit onto Route 519 north. Drive north about 4.2 miles on Route 519, turn right (north) onto Route 647 (Harmony Brass Castle Road). From there, keep track of the mile markers and turn right

Check for woodpecker activity in the dead trees that rim the reservoir.

onto Montana Road just past Mile Marker 5. Two miles down the road will be a T; turn right onto Richline Road and drive 0.7 mile to the entrance of the preserve. This is not necessarily the quickest way, but it is the easiest (and safest) way to get there. Signs at the entrance will direct you to the visitor center, or follow the boat launch signs straight ahead to go directly to the ramp.

From the north, drive south on Route 647 from Route 623, a few miles south of Oxford. Keep track of the mile markers and slow down as you near Mile Marker 5. Montana Road will be on your left, just before you get to Mile Marker 5. Continue as above. New Jersey Division of Fish and Wildlife, Northern Region Office, 26 Route 173 West, Hampton, NJ 08827; 973-383-0918.

Lakes Hopatcong and Musconectong
Lake Hopatcong and Netcong (Morris/Sussex)

Lake Hopatcong is the largest natural lake in the state, covering 2,685 acres and more than 40 miles of shoreline. Is it pretty? Well, it's definitely very impressive. There are some charming spots, but houses and marinas pack the shoreline for most of its length. On weekends in the summer, it's a veritable zoo, with fishing tournaments, sailing regattas, and the like. I understand from locals that during the week, even in August, it's pretty quiet on the water. There is no limit on the size of gas motors, hence, the waters can churn up wildly from boats on weekends. At some point you should paddle it, preferably during the week, just to feel and absorb its expansiveness and to imagine how breathtaking it was for the Native Americans who looked down on the waters from the surrounding hillsides. The name Hopatcong is derived from the Lenni Lenapi Indian word *huppakong*, meaning "honey waters of many coves."

Great for fishing, Lake Hopatcong boasts rainbow and brown trout, hybrid bass, crappie, walleye, pickerel, largemouth and small-mouth bass, perch, sunfish, and other species. Supposedly the coves are prime habitat for bass. A glacial lake left by the last Ice Age, winter snows now refurbish the waters that are cold even in summer. Be adequately prepared with additional clothing when you paddle here. Public access to the lake is provided through Lake Hopatcong State Park on Route 631 on the southwest end of the lake. A public beach is next to the concrete boat ramp and restroom facilities are near the entrance booth. A small entrance fee is charged during the summer.

An alternate public access to the lake is through Lee County Park, a third of the way up the lake on the eastern side. A small fee is charged to launch your boat, even in the off-season. Since the extreme northern

end of the lake is more scenic and slightly less populated, launching from here puts you a few miles closer.

Lake Musconectong (a Native American word for "rapidly running river") is only a short drive away from the southern end of Lake Hopatcong. Though much smaller at only 328 acres, I personally preferred this lake and found it more scenic and relaxing. A state park of the same name provides a narrow border of woods around the entire lake in the little town of Netcong.

Camping is available at the Mahlon Dickerson Reservation off Exit 34B of I-80. Take Route 15 north 5.0 miles to the Weldon Road exit and drive east on Weldon Road 3.5 miles. This is a 3,000-acre county park with wooded sites. Mahlon Dickerson Reservation, P.O. Box 684, Lake Hopatcong, NJ 07849; 973-663-0200. Open year-round.

You have to try Lake Hopatcong at least once, but paddle the waters midweek unless you enjoy wakes from motorboats.

An early morning mist rises from Lake Musconectong.

Getting there

To Lake Hopatcong: Drive north 1.2 miles on Route 631 (Landing Road) from Exit 28 off I-80. At the junction of Routes 631 and 607, Route 631 turns left. Stay to your right and drive 0.4 mile north on Route 607. The park entrance will be on your right. The state park is so popular that signs leading to it are everywhere—if you miss them, see your optometrist. Lake Hopatcong State Park, P.O. Box 8519, Landing, NJ 07850; 973-398-7010.

To Lee County Park: Take Exit 30 (Mount Arlington) from I-80 and drive north 3.6 miles on Route 615 (Howard Boulevard) to the entrance of Lee County Park on the left. Pay the inexpensive launch fee at the booth on the dock to the left.

To Lake Musconectong: If you're going to Lake Musconectong because Lake Hopatcong State Park is filled, drive 0.4 mile south on Route 607 from the park entrance, turn right onto Route 631 south (Center Street) and drive 1.6 miles. To the right of the large "Welcome to Netcong" sign between the road and the lake, a long parking area parallels the road. Pull into the parking area and launch from the south end, where a clearing to the lake is provided. New Jersey Division of Fish and Wildlife, Northern Region Office, 26 Route 173 West, Hampton, NJ, 08827; 973-383-0918.

Silver Lake
Franklin (Sussex)

It isn't big, but Silver Lake is charming and relaxing. Part of a New Jersey Fish and Game area, this cozy lake of approximately 20 acres is located on the outskirts of Fawn Lake, a quiet little community adjacent to Hamburg Mountain Wildlife Management Area. Densely forested game lands encircle the lake and a small, shrub-covered rocky island on the south end provides a great picnic spot in a tranquil setting. This isn't a place where one can spend an entire afternoon exploring, yet you could easily spend an hour or more observing and photographing the abundant bird life as you paddle slowly around the lake. If you're lucky, you might spot a raccoon. I saw several sets of tracks around the sandy launch site, and several deer trails led into the lake. Only electric outboards are allowed, guaranteeing a quiet paddle.

If you're in the area, complete the day with visits to the famous Franklin Mines, Franklin Museum, and several gem shops in the nearby town of Franklin. Rocks in this region of New Jersey have gone through dramatic geological changes as the plates below the earth's crust collided over millions of years to form the Appalachian Mountains. This process resulted in the formation of more than a hundred different minerals, many of which have not been discovered anywhere else in the world. Franklinite, a black, zinc-iron oxide mineral, was named after the town and has only been found in Franklin and the neighboring town of Ogdensburg.

Mine tours make a great adventure for children, as they put on a miner's helmet and walk through tunnels while a guide talks about mining operations and the various minerals found there. In the gem shops, children usually go right for pyrite, a heavy mineral known as "fool's gold" because of its glistening resemblance in color and weight to the real thing.

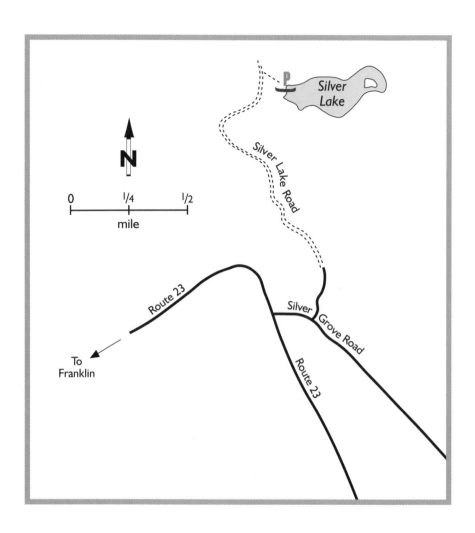

Camping is available at Beaver Hill Campground in Sussex about 16.0 miles away. From Route 23, drive south 1.0 mile on I-94, turn right and drive west 2.0 miles on Route 661 (Beaver Run Road). Turn left onto Big Spring Road for 0.5 mile. The campground will be on your left. Beaver Hill Campground, P.O. Box 353, Sussex, NJ 07461; 973-827-0670.

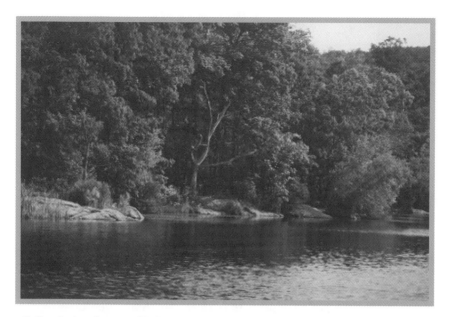

Solitude is what you'll find at this quaint little lake near Hamburg Mountain.

Getting there

From Route 631 (Franklin Avenue), drive south 3.0 miles on Route 23 and turn left onto Silver Grove Road. A small bridge crosses over a railroad track immediately after you turn. Silver Grove Road forks 0.1 mile past the railroad tracks. Take the left fork, which will be Silver Lake Road, and drive 0.2 mile to the small sign for Silver Lake. From the sign, the rickety road becomes very narrow, more one-lane than two-lane, so drive the next 1.4 miles carefully. Turn right at the New Jersey Fish and Game sign and continue another 400 feet to the casual launch site and parking area. New Jersey Division of Fish and Wildlife, Northern Region Office, 26 Route 173 West, Hampton, NJ 08827; 973-383-0918.

Cranberry Lake
Cranberry Lake (Sussex)

The 180-acre Cranberry Lake is almost cut in half by a long, narrow peninsula barely attached on its western side, giving more shoreline to explore. Cranberry Lake Park on the northeast corner of the lake provides a boat launch, limited parking, and a hiking trail that travels along the stone dike edging the lake's southeastern shore. While you're there, examine the boulders that line the parking area for black, oblong hornblende crystals. Look for the shiny, sheetlike mineral black muscovite, which appears to have an oily sheen over its surface.

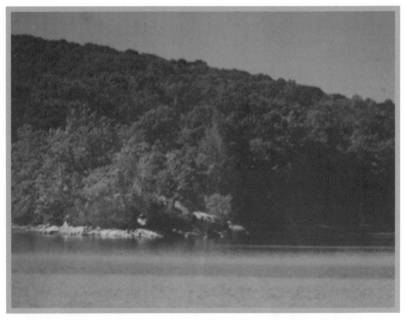

A rock outcropping in Allamuchy Mountain State Park cradles a small cove.

Saving the best for last, start your trip to the right (north) of the launch and paddle around the northern half of the lake. Once you're around the peninsula on the western side, you'll find the most remote and prettiest paddling as you enter the southern half of the lake, where mountains rise sharply. Allamuchy Mountain State Park grips the southern end of Cranberry Lake with tenacious fingers, cradling quiet coves that beg you to stop paddling, close your eyes, and breathe in the fresh mountain air of this tranquil hideaway.

Getting there

From Route 607, drive 3.2 miles north on Route 206, turn left onto South Shore Road, and drive 0.2 mile. A Cranberry Lake Park sign will be on your right. The right turn onto the gravel road is a very sharp hairpin turn that goes up a short but steep embankment. At the top of the embankment, turn right. Limited parking is immediately to your right. The concrete boat launch is down the road about 150 feet. You don't need to use the ramp if you can portage your kayak over the small guardrail and across the narrow dirt and stone dike to the water. New Jersey Division of Fish and Wildlife, Northern Region Office, 26 Route 173 West, Hampton, NJ 08827; 973-383-0918.

Muskrat
(Ondatra zibethica)

Semi-aquatic rodents, muskrats live in and around lakes, ponds, fresh- and saltwater marshes, and slow-moving streams throughout North America. Their common name is derived from the musk glands predominant beneath the skin on the lower abdomen of males, which produce a strong scent. Averaging two feet in length, the dark gray or brown fur of the muskrat fools many people into thinking they've spotted a beaver. A muskrat's partially webbed hind feet act as paddles, and its long, scaly, hairless tail, flattened sideways, acts as a rudder in the water. Mainly nocturnal, you can best see them at dawn or dusk, when they leave their burrow to feed on aquatic plants. Although primarily vegetarians preferring cattails, arrowhead weed, pondweed, bulbs, and tubers, they will occasionally dine on snails, crayfish, frogs, and carrion when plants are scarce. Muskrats clean all their food, washing it before consumption.

In marshlands, muskrats build dome-shaped houses as large as six to eight feet across and two feet high using reeds, Phragmites, and mud. Check channel corners as you paddle by for chewed off reeds, the telltale sign that a muskrat lives nearby—probably within 150 feet. Houses are located near the water, where an extensive tunnel system leads to several underwater entrances. In tidal waters, lakes, and slow-moving streams with steep banks they will sometimes make their homes by burrowing into the bank, and a small dome is built only for a surface entrance. Reeds and grasses line the main room above the high-water line. Muskrats construct special food huts near the main hut to store vegetative roots and grasses to use while nursing or during bad weather.

Breeding takes place from late March through July, producing an average of four litters of five to seven young each year. Although muskrats do not mate for life, they are thought to have only one mate during rearing seasons. Gestation lasts about a month, and babies are weaned by two months of age. Self-regulating animals, population density, habitat quality, and food availability affects the number and size of litters in a given year. Usually a solitary animal, except when mating, muskrats often share a communal den during the winter. They are prey for fox, hawks, raccoons, coyotes, and owls.

Large populations of muskrats can be deleterious to the aquatic vegetation necessary for other wildlife, and their burrowing activities weaken dikes and earthen dams. On the commercial scale, muskrats are valued for their fur and are often referred to as "river mink."

Splitrock Reservoir
Marcella (Morris)

Coming out of the local diner after breakfast, I asked a police officer about the paddling sites I intended to investigate that day. After looking over my list, he told me that Splitrock Reservoir, previously owned by the Jersey City Water Works, had been turned over to the state. It is scheduled to open to the public sometime in the summer of 2001. Call the Morris County Parks and Recreation office at 973-627-7200 to confirm the date before venturing out. It would be wise to keep abreast of this reservoir, as few will be aware of it initially and paddling conditions will be superb. Hope to see you there.

Splitrock Reservoir will be spectacular to paddle when it opens in the summer of 2001.

Compared to other reservoirs, Splitrock appears to be about 400 acres and, from what I could see from the road crossing the dam, it's absolutely gorgeous. My topographic map showed a few islands in the northern half, which should be very picturesque, but they were around the bend and out of site from my vantage point. Dense upland forests stand atop rocky shores around this remote body of water. Birch, maple, tulip, and sassafras trees were prominent near the dam.

Getting there

In Rockaway, take Exit 37 off I-80, drive north 6.4 miles on Route 513 (Green Pond Road). Turn right onto Upper Hibernia Road and drive 1.0 mile (curves sharply to the right at 0.3 mile) and turn left onto Splitrock Road. From there, go 1.0 mile to the dam at the southern end of the reservoir. Splitrock Road will change from blacktop to potholed gravel within a short distance. I suspect that the launch site will be somewhere along that road—they may even repave the road. When you call to find out if it is officially open, also inquire about launching facilities and any minimum length requirements for canoes and kayaks. Morris County Parks and Recreation, 53 East Hanover Avenue, Morristown, NJ 07962; 973-627-7200.

Central New Jersey

Northwest of an imaginary line running approximately from Trenton on the Delaware River to New Brunswick on the Atlantic Ocean, start the rolling hills of the Piedmont Plateau that grade into the higher mountains of northwestern New Jersey. Southeast of that line, the rolling hills gently flatten into a low coastal plain. Barrier islands rim the Atlantic Ocean like a necklace and help protect developed coastal areas from pounding ocean waves. The gravel and sand of the coastal plain gradually become dirt rich with minerals, on which horse and agricultural farms flourish. Valleys become natural holding basins for rainwater and small streams. Slightly cooler weather in the hills creates the southern extent of northern birds, such as the bobolink, which rarely make it south of Trenton during the summer.

The Delaware and Raritan Canal connects the Delaware River with the Raritan River, which flows into Raritan Bay on the Atlantic Ocean. This historic route once provided essential passage for the transportation of coal and other cargo from Pennsylvania to New York City and other towns along the Eastern Seaboard between 1834 and 1932. Mules plodded along the towpath beside the canal, pulling barges laden with goods on a two-day journey from Bordentown to New Brunswick. Many historically designated bridge-tenders' houses and hand-laid cobblestone spillways along the canal offer a glimpse of the era before railroads replaced water as an economic and efficient mode of transportation. The canal and towpath are now part of the National Recreational Trail System.

Delaware and Raritan Canal
South Bound Brook to Griggstown (Sussex)

Ask anyone who paddles the Delaware and Raritan Canal, and they'll tell you they think it more a narrow lake than a river. Overflow culverts drain excessive water from the canal into nearby waterways such as the Raritan and Millstone Rivers, thus retaining a slow flow rate throughout the canal's length. In times of insufficient rain, water is pumped into the canal from these same nearby rivers. The original canal, which ran from Bordentown to New Brunswick, was 44 miles long and 70 feet wide. A 13-mile feeder canal, which provided water for the current, ran from Bull's Island on the Delaware River above Raven Rock to Trenton. Today approximately 36 miles of the original canal remain intact along with 12 miles of the feeder canal. Around 70 million gallons of water per day from that system supplement the water supply of many communities in central New Jersey. The Green Acres Program has efforts underway to widen the current Delaware and Raritan Canal Park, which narrowly rims 70 miles of the main canal and feeder.

Quaint villages such as Griggstown and Blackwells Mills have retained their nineteenth century architecture, transporting you back in time as you glide past historic homes and under turn-of-the-century bridges. Joggers, bikers, and strollers enjoy the earthen towpath that parallels the canal as it winds its way past miles of fields and forests between towns. Trees burst with color in autumn when maple, sycamore, beech, and hickory display their finery before the onset of winter. You may have to duck a bit when passing under one or more of the old, low bridges that span the canal. Paddling up and back the waterway is easy, but this also would be the perfect opportunity to combine paddling with biking or hiking.

Griggstown is one of the more historic villages along the route and features a wooden canal bridge, Mule Tender's Barracks Canal Museum, a bridge-tender's house and station, and an old mill site.

Large, grassy fields with picnic tables and grills are within a short walking distance of the canal access. Spend the morning paddling the canal, have a picnic lunch, then visit the bridge-tender's house in the afternoon to get a glimpse into the lives of those who once lived there. Canoes can be rented in Griggstown from private concessionaires.

Along Blackwells Mills, another charming village, you'll find a bridge-tender's house, a rickety wooden bridge, and an old mill site along the canal. Picnic tables and grills are located around a large field with views of the river.

Getting there

Numerous designated parking lots with boat access are next to the tow-path along the canal. I have only listed a few, chosen for their historic settings and scenic waters.

To access the canal at Amwell and Blackwells Mills: From Route 206, drive east 3.6 miles on Route 514 (Amwell Road). After passing over the Millstone River, look for the parking lot on your left, on the west side of the canal in Amwell. Launch directly into the canal from there. You can paddle north 3.2 miles before encountering a lock. To get to Blackwells Mills, continue on Route 514 across the canal, turn right onto Canal Road, and drive 2.2 miles to Blackwells Mills Road. Turn right and cross over the canal. Launch from the west side of the canal, and park your car in the large parking lot on the left, about 100 feet down the hill from the canal.

The park office is located at Blackwells Mills. From Route 514, drive south 2.1 miles on Route 533 (Millstone River Road). Turn left onto Blackwells Mills Road and drive 0.2 mile. Turn right onto Canal Road and drive about 100 feet to the office on the left.

Delaware and Raritan Canal Park, 625 Canal Road, Somerset, NJ 08873; 732-873-3050.

Caution: Avoid the canal that parallels the Delaware River, as the current runs too swift for a two-way trip and can even be dangerous in times of high water. You could store your bike at a lock farther south, but the nonstop traffic along Route 29 offsets some of the aesthetics of paddling between the quaint towns of Lambertville, Stockton, and Washington's Crossing. If you choose to paddle it, be prepared to go elsewhere if the water is too turbulent.

Lake Surprise
Mountainside (Union)

The aptly named Lake Surprise, a quaint 25-acre lake, was a surprise to find in the midst of heavily populated towns. Located in a ravine within the 2,000-acre Watchung Reservation, hemlock and pine are interspersed with beech, maple, locust, and other hardwoods around the lake. The reservation hosts numerous activities, including horseback riding, hiking, an environmental activity center, a butterfly garden, picnic groves, and a planetarium.

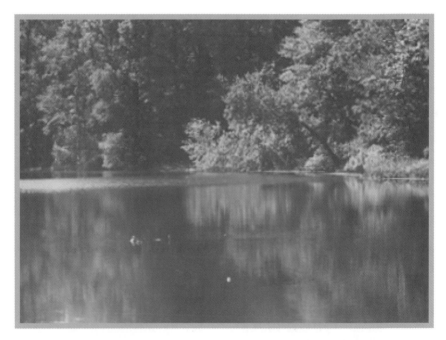

Lake Surprise is situated at the bottom of a ravine in the Watchung Mountains.

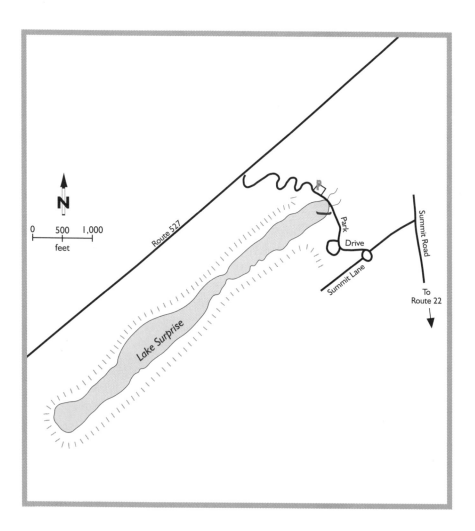

At 1.0-mile long and 100-feet wide, the lake will not provide a long paddle, but the setting is gorgeous—perfect for a quick trip at the end of a hectic day and ideal for the novice. Lake depth averages four feet, with a number of spots on the southwest end reaching eight feet. Painted and spotted turtles, butterflies, and birds are its main wildlife. Miles of hiking trails take you up and down mountainous terrain, where you're likely to encounter deer, fox, and skunk.

Getting there

From Route 22, take the Watchung Reservation/Summit Road exit near the town of Mountainside. Drive 1.2 miles west on Summit Road, turn left onto Summit Lane, and drive 0.8 mile. At the circle, make the first right—there will be a sign pointing toward the lake. Stay to the right on the main road for 1.2 miles to the lake. Launch from the east side of the bridge (as you approach the lake) and park in the lot on the west side of the bridge 50 feet up the road. Trailside Nature and Science Center, 452 New Providence Road, Mountainside, NJ 07092; 908-789-3670.

Lakes Carasaljo and Shenandoah
Lakewood (Ocean)

It was a pleasure to find two nice lakes to paddle in a densely populated town rife with industrial parks. Long and narrow, Lake Carasaljo's 70 acres is bordered almost completely by a wide, lightly wooded swath of municipal park. Bikers, joggers, and walkers make their way along a trail on the southern shore that weaves through the trees along the shoreline. A small, sandy swimming beach is located midway on the north side. The best paddling is on the western half, away from Route 9. Depending on water levels, you may be able to paddle up Carasaljo River at the extreme western end of the lake for a 0.5-mile or more.

Lake Shenandoah County Park was once part of John D. Rockefeller's vacation estate, to which hemlock and unique specimen trees were imported from all over the country. More than 140 acres of park offer biking and hiking trails, a small picnic area, and restrooms. Dense woods to the south, east, and northeast surround the park's 50-acre lake. On the northwest side, tall grasses give way to dense shrubs and saplings, a perfect habitat for box turtles and black racers, a fast-moving, satiny black snake. Two islands halfway down the lake add a spark of interest to your trip. Though Lake Shenandoah may be a little smaller, its location on the outskirts of town makes this a better paddle.

Getting there

To Lake Carasaljo: From the south, drive north on Route 9 from Route 70. At the Route 628 junction, continue north 0.7 mile on Route 9 to Central Avenue. Turn left onto Central Avenue and make an immediate right onto South Lake Drive. Drive 0.9 mile to the stone launch site and parking area on your right.

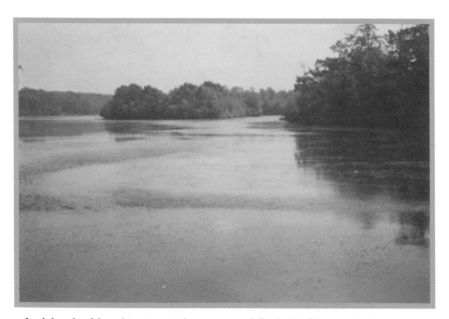

An island adds adventure when you paddle Lake Shenandoah.

From the north, take Route 9 south to Main Street in Lakewood—a sign for Route 528 east is on the left. Continue south on Route 9 two blocks, passing the lake on your right, and turn right onto Central Avenue. Continue as above.

To Lake Shenandoah: From Route 9, drive east 1.0 mile on Route 528 (Cedar Bridge Avenue), turn left onto South Clover Street, and drive 0.5 mile to the park entrance on your right. The boat ramp and parking area are right inside the entrance. New Jersey Division of Fish and Wildlife, Central Region (Assunpink WMA), 386 Clarksburg-Robbinsville Road, Robbinsville, NJ 08691; 609-259-2132.

Osprey
(Pandion haliaetus)

For years, the osprey population suffered a decline, due in large part to pesticides and habitat destruction. With the help of artificial nesting sites and a ban on DDT, they are making a tremendous comeback. Also known as "fish hawks," they are the only bird of prey (raptor) whose front talons turn backward and the only one that plunges feet first into the water. Spines on the osprey's toes enable it to hold on to slippery fish, its main prey. These birds are known to hunt the occasional small rodent or crustacean when fishing is poor.

Osprey favor open streams, rivers, and lakes, nesting in treetops near water. Brown above and white below, its most distinguishing field marks are its broad, black cheek patch and black wrist patches. The adult wingspan of an osprey averages 4 to 4.5 feet, and males are slightly smaller in size than females.

Females choose partners based on nest location, and the pair generally mate for life. Both adults help build the large stick nest, which measures three to five feet in diameter. While males and females may winter in different locations, they return to their nest within a few days of each other. Osprey arrive in southern New Jersey around the end of March and in northern New Jersey a week or two later. Courtship flights, a graceful touch-and-go aerial maneuver, can be seen the first week or two after their arrival, as mating pairs are made or renewed. Part of the mating ritual entails the male catching fish for the female, to prove he will be, or still is, a good provider.

From pairing until egg-laying, females are fed by the males. Both adults assist in repairing the old nest, shoring up walls with fresh twigs and lining the bottom with mucky sod. From my personal observations, both will bring in twigs but more often than not the female does the arranging.

When not hunting, the male can be found on his roost about a hundred yards away and within visual contact of the nest. At the first hint of danger, such as human intrusion or blackbird mobbing, the female emits a high-pitched *eep, eep, eep* sound, a signal for the male to come flying to the rescue. As the female nears egg-laying time, she stays closer to the nest, leaving infrequently to stretch her wings. Once the eggs (two to four) are laid, she hunkers down in the nest, with only the top of her head visible to a careful observer. The female incubates the eggs and will trade off periodically with the male. After catching a fish, the male eats the head and neck area, then brings the remainder to the nest and takes over incubation while the female feeds. After the female has eaten and preened, she resumes incubation and the male returns to his proximal roost.

Their young hatch about five weeks after the eggs are laid, but it will take an additional seven to eight weeks until they are ready to leave the nest. Even then, the parents must provide food for the first few weeks until the young can hunt well enough on their own. Catching fish through the warped air-water interface evidently requires practice, practice, and more practice. By mid-October, osprey start heading south to their favorite wintering ground.

Manasquan Reservoir
Glendora (Monmouth)

The 720-acre Manasquan Reservoir will keep you paddling for hours. Outboard and canoe rentals are available on the lower level of the visitor center next to the boat ramp. The upper level of the visitor center houses a food concession, operated only during summer months, as well as environmental displays and an observation deck. Horseback riding is available and a jogging/biking path extends around the reservoir's perimeter. Numerous hiking trails meander through the woods.

Dainty asters sprinkle the lakeside in late summer.

Manasquan Reservoir

dike

dike

Windeler Road

Georgia Tavern Road

Route 9

195

N

0   1/4   1/2
       mile

Turn right from the launch to paddle past a cove filled with dead trees bleached silvery gray from the sun. Woodpeckers occasionally tap their way into the hollow core of the taller dead trees in early summer. Reportedly, fishing is excellent, particularly for crappie, bass, and trout. There is a nominal boat ramp fee year-round and a park entrance fee in summer.

Getting there

From Route 9 at the junction of I-195, drive north 0.2 mile on Route 9. Turn right onto Georgia Tavern Road and drive 0.4 mile, then turn right onto Windeler Road (there is a sign for Manasquan Reservoir at Windeler Road). Drive 2.0 miles to the park entrance on your left and follow signs to the boat launch. New Jersey Division of Fish and Wildlife, Central Region (Assunpink WMA), 386 Clarksburg-Robbinsville Road, Robbinsville, NJ 08691; 609-259-2132.

Prospertown Lake
Prospertown (Ocean)

Hours of paddling can be enjoyed in this remote yet easily accessible location surrounded by Prospertown Wildlife Management Area. Neither gas nor electric motors are permitted, but since the lake is not patrolled regularly, a few tend to slip in now and then. Nevertheless, these waters rarely become crowded, even on the hottest summer weekend. A narrow stretch of open sandy beach near the launch can get a bit busy at dusk, when local anglers come try their luck for an hour or two. If you paddle toward the extreme northeast end, you'll find yourself entering grounds owned by Six Flags Great Adventure Park. No, you won't be permitted to land on their property; guards continually patrol that section. Though located near this popular attraction, traffic on Route 537 by the lake is minimal in this sparsely populated area of the state.

A few small islands break up the lake's surface close to shore by the bend in the northeast section. Inlets and coves of all sizes provide excellent habitat for turtles, deer, raccoons, beaver, and waterfowl. Painted and spotted turtles are a common sight on sunny shores and logs, while low grasses around the launch site harbor garter snakes. Around the bend to the northeast, a picturesque area of silvery-smooth dead trees provide a prime habitat for woodpeckers. Hawks and vultures frequent the skies above the lake while blue jays and songbirds delight in the pristine habitat of dense beech, hickory, and hardwood forests.

Water depth in this 80-acre lake extends to about 21 feet, the deeper portions found closer to the side opposite the launch. Bass, catfish, sunfish, and crappie are the most sought-after species by anglers.

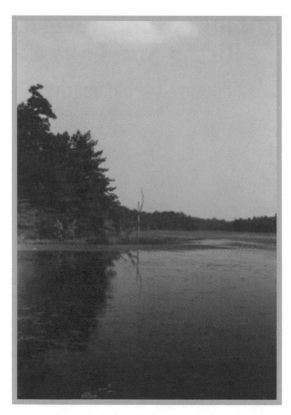

Large populations of spotted and painted turtles live in Prospertown Lake.

Getting there

Prospertown Lake is conveniently located just off Route 537, approximately 2.6 miles south of Exit 16 off I-195. Millers Mill Road is exactly at Mile Marker 39 on the west side of Route 537. The entrance to the lake is about 200 feet south of Mile Marker 39 on the left. A sign designating the entrance to the lake is clearly visible. New Jersey Division of Fish and Wildlife, Central Region (Assunpink WMA), 386 Clarksburg-Robbinsville Road, Robbinsville, NJ 08691; 609-259-2132.

Assunpink, Stone Tavern, and Rising Sun Lakes
Roosevelt (Monmouth)

Get out here and paddle! More than 5,000 acres of Wildlife Management Area surround three beautiful lakes: 225-acre Lake Assunpink, 52-acre Stone Tavern Lake, and 38-acre Rising Sun Lake. Each lake has its own character, its own special charm. With its large size and numerous coves and inlets, Lake Assunpink offers more hours of paddling pleasure. Although never very crowded, anglers frequent this lake on summer weekends looking for bass and pickerel.

The sun spreads its rays over flat waters at day's end.

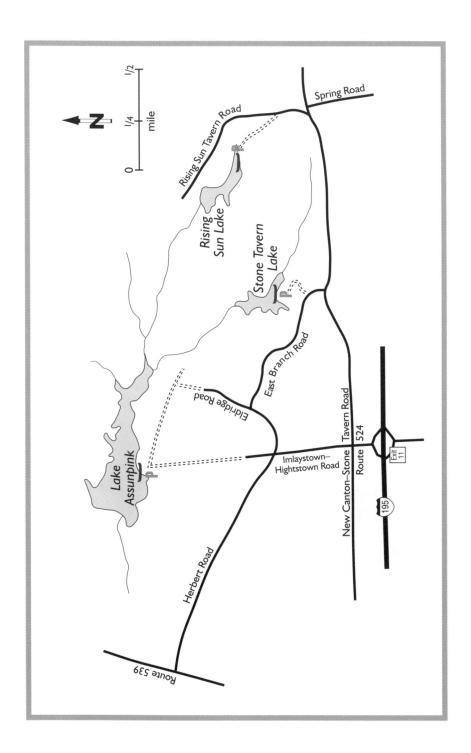

Sweetgum, pine, red maple, and oak dominate the surrounding woods behind a screen of cattails, Phragmites, mulberry bushes, and joe-pye weed bordering the lakes.

Joe-pye weed (*Eupatorium maculatum*) was used extensively by Native Americans to cure renal problems, especially kidney stones, and fevers. Reputed Native American healer Joe Pye lived in colonial New England and used this herb to cure typhoid and other fevers. During late summer, the plant develops purplish-brown clusters of flowers that add a soft touch of color to swampy borders.

Stone Tavern Lake is smaller but more nestled in the woods and very tranquil. Cast your eyes skyward occasionally to spot one of the many red-tail hawks that frequent the area as you explore the lake's numerous coves. Wild blueberry and fragrant sweet pepperbush nudge their way into the dappled sunlight. Rising Sun Lake, the smallest of the three, sits among woods and open fields. Only electric motors are permitted on the lakes, assuring a quiet paddle.

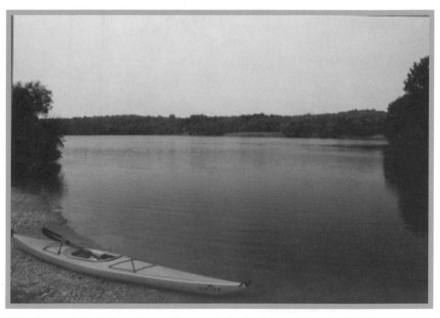

Far from civilization, Stone Tavern Lake invites you to paddle its tranquil waters.

Getting there

To Lake Assunpink: Take I-195 to Exit 11 (Hightstown/Imlaystown). Drive north 2.6 miles toward Hightstown on Imlaystown-Hightstown Road to the T, turn left, and drive 100 feet to the huge parking and launch area. The road becomes sand for the last 1.3 miles after crossing Herbert/East Branch Road.

To Stone Tavern Lake: From Imlaystown-Hightstown Road, drive 1.8 miles east on East Branch Road (it will make a right bend 0.5 mile into the drive). You will pass a narrow dirt road on the left (north) about 150 feet before the gray-stone entrance road, also on the left. Drive 0.4 mile to the lake; there is parking for about ten cars and a launch from the sandy beach.

To Rising Sun Lake: From Imlaystown-Hightstown Road just north of I-195, drive 3.2 miles east on Route 524 (New Canton-Stone Tavern Road). Turn left (north) on Route 571 (Rising Sun Tavern Road) and drive 1.3 miles to the dirt entrance road on the left (west). Parking and the dirt launch are about 200 feet ahead. New Jersey Division of Fish and Wildlife, Central Region (Assunpink WMA), 386 Clarksburg-Robbinsville Road, Robbinsville, NJ 08691; 609-259-2132.

Forge Pond
Brick (Ocean)

Forty-five acres are yours to enjoy in the midst of this bustling city. During the day, egrets, blue herons, songbirds, box and painted turtles, and huge snapping turtles are plentiful. An occasional water snake may be spotted slithering along the surface. The serene pond area is historically where the Lenni Lenape Indians met and performed their rituals, spring through fall. From the pond, you can paddle under the Route 70 bridge and onto the Metedeconk River. There is a mild tidal current as Forge Pond flows into Barnegat Bay, about 3.5 miles down the narrow river. The river is surrounded for a short distance by a wildlife area to the south and a residential shore to the north, where it widens, and becomes choppier. Only electric outboards are permitted on the pond, but if you enter the Metedeconk River, anything goes.

Getting there

At the horrendous junction of Routes 88 and 70, turn east onto Route 70 and drive 0.3 mile to the entrance, which is beside a small strip mall. Parking is available for about ten cars.

Shadow Lake
Red Bank (Monmouth)

It is like a fairy tale. Tucked away neatly at the bottom of a steep hill in Stevenson Park, the dirt launch at Shadow Lake faces thickly wooded, steep hills surrounding its western half. Though half of the northern shore and part of the southern are privately owned, you'd never guess it as most of the houses sit near the top of steep hills deep within the thick woods. Only when you get close to the dam on the lake's eastern end will civilization become more visible. A dirt road leads off from the

Swans glide among a carpet of water lilies in the shallow terminus of Shadow Lake.

park down a winding passage to the lake, where underbrush has been cleared in a small area to accommodate a few picnic tables.

Pine, beech, hickory, maple, and ash march up the steep hills overlooking waters inhabited by sunfish, smallmouth and largemouth bass, trout, and pickerel. Depth in this 88-acre lake averages 15 feet, with depths to more than 30 feet on the eastern end closer to the dam. To the right of the launch, where a stream enters the lake, ducks and geese share a carpet of white and yellow pond lilies with painted turtles and frogs. Part of that small, shallow area is private property and posted prominently as such.

Getting there

From southbound Garden State Parkway take Exit 109, turn left at end of ramp, and drive 0.3 mile east on Route 520 (Newman Springs Road). Turn left onto Half Mile Road and drive 0.6 mile. Turn left onto West Front Street and drive 0.5 mile. A sign is on the right for Stevenson Park. Turn right into the park (Shady Oak Way) and drive 0.2 mile. Turn right immediately past the small bridge over the creek onto the dirt road. The launch site is about 100 feet down on the right.

From northbound Garden State Parkway, take Exit 109. As you come down the exit ramp, stay left, watching for signs for Half Mile Road that will be straight ahead of you at the bottom of the ramp. Cross Route 520 onto Half Mile Road and proceed as above. New Jersey Division of Fish and Wildlife, Central Region (Assunpink WMA), 386 Clarksburg-Robbinsville Road, Robbinsville, NJ 08691; 609-259-2132.

Round Valley Reservoir
Lebanon (Hunterdon)

At 2,350 acres, Round Valley is the state's largest reservoir and its second largest body of freshwater, surpassed only by Lake Hopatcong. It is also one of the most heavily fished waters in the region. The reservoir opened in 1972 as a backup to nearby Spruce Run and its shape is primarily—you guessed it—round. As with Merrill Creek and Spruce Run, a warning light flashes from a tower when winds become 25 MPH for five seconds or more, requiring all boats to head back to the launch. Other than a concrete dam to the left of the launch, mixed-oak hardwood forests with an occasional thick stand of pines hug the shoreline.

Leaving behind the busy launch area, paddle to your right around the small peninsula, where the waters open wide. Shallow coves and small points of land break up the shoreline for an interesting paddle, but don't forget to check the sky occasionally for bald eagles searching for a meal. Hawks and vultures circle in the thermals of air above the lake; warblers, kingfishers, blue jays, finches, and other songbirds flit in and about the trees along the water.

I paddled the perimeter of the reservoir with two local kayakers who advised hugging the shores on weekends between Independence Day and Labor Day. Evidently, the central waters can become crazed with anglers. One kayaker who paddles here often mentioned that he sees eagles plunge for fish "at least once each summer." Take advantage of camping facilities in the park around the time of a full moon and enjoy relaxing moonlight paddles—but don't forget a waterproof flashlight and an emergency strobe.

Bring fishing equipment along if you'd like, as Round Valley is well-known for its excellent fishing. Largemouth and smallmouth bass, brown and rainbow trout, yellow and white perch (great panfish), and large sunfish all inhabit the waters, which reach a depth of 175 feet.

This is the only lake in New Jersey with a population of reproducing lake trout.

Wilderness family campsites, some accessible only by boat, highlight an extended trip. Miles of hiking and biking trails pass through hemlock valleys and hardwood highlands. The park is open 24 hours a day, 365 days a year, and ramp access is free. Boating is prohibited at the recreation lake, which is accessible through the park's main entrance for those who wish to enjoy the beach, playground, and large picnic area. A fee is charged in summer.

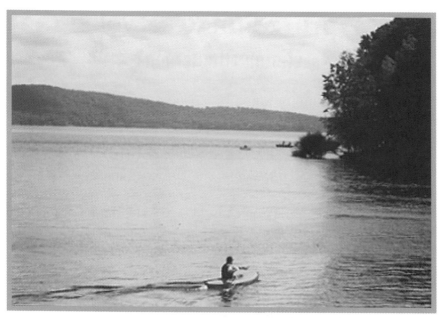

A kayaker paddles out to explore the vast waters of Round Valley Reservoir and try his luck at fishing.

Getting there

From the east, take I-78 west to Exit 20 toward Lebanon/Round Valley Recreation Area. It will merge into Route 639 south (Cokesbury Road). Drive 0.3 mile to the T at Main Street. Turn left and drive 0.1 mile to Route 629 (Cherry Street). Turn right and drive 1.4 miles to the boat launch entrance road on the left. If you continue another 0.9 mile, you'll find the entrance to the small recreational lake (no boating) with a beach, picnic grove, and a playground.

From the west, take I-78 east to Exit 18 (Lebanon/Route 22 east). Follow Route 22 east for 1.6 miles, veer right onto Main Street, drive 0.6 mile to Route 629 (Cherry Street), and continue as above. Large signs are posted all along the roads for a 5.0-mile radius around the reservoir, making it impossible to miss. Round Valley Recreation Area, Box 45D, Lebanon Stanton Road, Lebanon, NJ 08833; 908-236-6355.

Spruce Run Reservoir
Clinton (Hunterdon)

Built in 1965 for the Elizabethtown Water Company, the highly irregular outline of this 1,300-acre reservoir resembles a serpentine monster. You could spend a week paddling in and out of all the little nooks and crannies. In my opinion, this is the most interesting of the three area reservoirs, even though it's only half the size of Round Valley.

Plan to camp here for a day or two to fully explore all the coves and peninsulas.

Campsites are available on the grounds, inviting you to spend a few rewarding days. Make reservations ahead of time to assure availability.

Clinton Wildlife Management Area and Spruce Run State Park surround most of the reservoir, offering thousands of acres of forest for hiking and biking. I found the most picturesque paddling to the south and southwest, where coves and peninsulas are most abundant and give you a better chance for solitude on crowded summer weekends. Hunterdon Sailing Club is based at the park and commonly holds regattas and other sailing events on weekends throughout the summer. Best bet for a secluded trip is to visit here off-season or on weekdays in summer.

Eagles, hawks, vultures, snakes, skunk, deer, fox, and raccoons inhabit the forested lands. Along the tree-lined shores, you'll find numerous songbirds, bobolinks, blue jays, and warblers flitting about the branches overhanging the waters. Hybrid bass, pike, trout, and perch can be found in these waters that extend down to 75 feet. I understand that hybrid bass give you a thrilling fight. While not an avid angler, I do take a fishing pole along a few times each year. Perhaps one day I'll hook a hybrid.

Access to the boat launch is through Spruce Run State Park off Van Syckel's Corner Road. A modest fee is charged to enter the main park in the summer. The park is open 24 hours a day, 365 days a year. Outboard motors are limited to ten horsepower.

Getting there

Take Exit 12 off I-78 and turn north onto Route 635. Drive 1.1 miles, turn right onto Van Syckel's Corner Road, and drive 2.0 miles to the park's entrance on the right. Spruce Run State Park, One Van Syckel's Corner Road, Clinton, NJ 08809; 908-638-8572.

Lake Mercer
West Windsor (Mercer)

Mercer County Park is a huge complex located midway between Princeton and Trenton. The park's miles of rolling hills sprinkled with trees and woods have something for everyone, including golf, soccer, tennis, and, of course, boating. Set in the midst of the park is the 275-acre Lake Mercer with launch facilities, a small nature center, and restrooms. University sculling crews practice on the lake and anglers come from miles around to try their luck. While most water activities occur in the central and western parts of the lake, the best paddling can be found on the eastern end, where thick woods line the shores. If you

Canada geese fly over an angler heading toward his favorite spot.

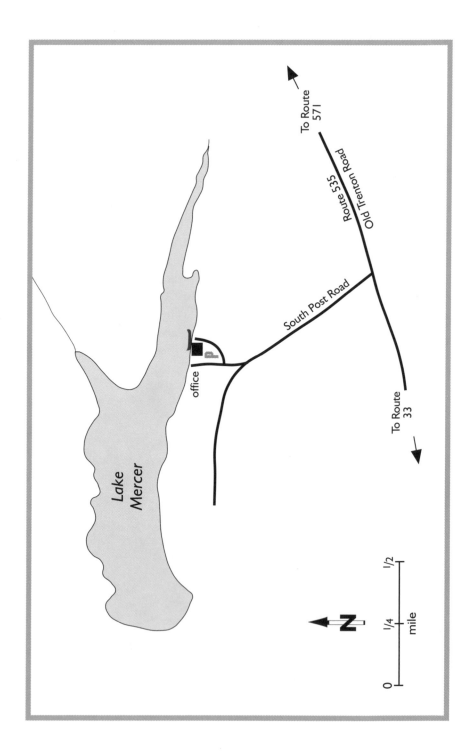

live around this highly populated area and want some large waters to paddle without traveling too far, this is the place.

Getting there

From Route 571, drive south 3.9 miles on Route 535. Turn right (west) onto Route 602 (South Post Road) into the park entrance and drive 1.1 miles to the marina entrance on your right. Take the first right to the launch site. The lower level parking is for the big boats, the ones that need to be hauled by a trailer. After unloading your kayak or canoe, drive back up and around to the upper level parking lot.

From Route 33, drive north 3.8 miles on Route 535. Turn left (west) onto Route 602 (South Post Road) and continue as above. New Jersey Division of Fish and Wildlife, Central Region (Assunpink WMA), 386 Clarksburg-Robbinsville Road, Robbinsville, NJ 08691; 609-259-2132.

Lake Topanemus
Freehold (Monmouth)

This quaint little lake is tucked away from the bustling activity of Route 9, just north of Freehold. Large oak and maple provide dense shade in the picnic and launch area, where a few lakeside benches invite you to sit and enjoy the scenery. A hiking trail leading from the east end of the parking area takes you through the woods and around most of the lake. Some private property is across the lake from the launch, but the houses are set far back from the water. Launch your boat and head east (left) to enjoy an hour or more of lovely paddling along the wooded shores. Perhaps you'll pass painted or spotted turtles basking in the sun, or spot a kingfisher looking for dinner. The lake is stocked with largemouth bass that swim among channel catfish, bluegill sunfish, and fathead minnows.

Getting there

From Route 522, drive north 0.4 mile on Route 9, turn right (east), and drive 0.4 mile on Schibanoff Lane. Turn right (south) onto Waterworks Road and drive 0.1 mile. Turn left (east) onto Topanemus Lane, drive 0.2 mile, and turn left (north) onto Pond Road. Drive 0.5 mile to Lake Topanemus Park on the right. The stone boat ramp is about 100 feet farther on the right, with an informal parking area on the left. New Jersey Division of Fish and Wildlife, Central Region (Assunpink WMA), 386 Clarksburg-Robbinsville Road, Robbinsville, NJ 08691; 609-259-2132.

Route 9

Pond Road

P

Lake
Topanemus

Schibanoff Lane

Waterworks Road

Topanemus Lane

To
Route 522

N

0   1/4   1/2

mile

Farrington Lake
New Brunswick (Middlesex)

Created by damming the Passaic River, this long, narrow lake is bordered on both sides by county parklands, where hiking trails meander through landscaped trees and shrubs. In the midst of a large metropolis, the park and its 290-acre lake provide a pleasant sanctuary from traffic, crowds, and industry for humans and wildlife. Goldfinch, cardinals, wrens, warblers, blue jays, and other songbirds seek refuge among the trees, while sunfish, perch, and catfish swim in the waters alongside stocked trout and bass. Electric outboards are permitted, but most fishing is done from shore. There are two good launch sites with ample parking and nearby picnic tables.

Getting there

To the north launch from the New Jersey Turnpike, drive south 0.4 mile on Route 130. Turn left onto Farrington Boulevard and drive 0.4 mile to the parking area and launch.

To the central launch from the New Jersey Turnpike, drive south 1.7 miles on Route 130, turn left onto Washington Avenue, and drive 0.2 mile. A parking lot and launch site are right before the bridge. New Jersey Division of Fish and Wildlife, Central Region (Assunpink WMA), 386 Clarksburg-Robbinsville Road, Robbinsville, NJ 08691; 609-259-2132.

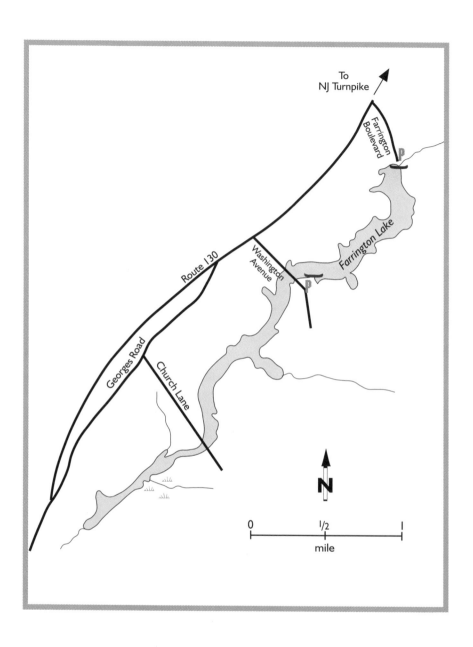

To
NJ Turnpike

Farrington Boulevard

P

Farrington Lake

Route 130

Washington Avenue

P

Georges Road

Church Lane

N

0   1/2   1
mile

Pitcher Plant
(Sarracenia purpurea)

The carnivorous pitcher plant's common name is derived from the unusual shape of its leaf and its capacity to hold water. Sandy wetland soils are high in iron but low in nitrogen and other essential nutrients. Unusual plants such as pitchers and sundews have developed insect-eating adaptations to augment the inadequate supply of nitrogen in poor soil conditions. Hollow leaves retain water and digestive juices that first lure, then kill and slowly absorb unwary insects. Internal hairs point downward to hinder the insect's escape. The plant's diet consists of flies, moths, gnats, ants, bees, small butterflies, and even an occasional tiny frog. Leaves vary from yellow-green to deep purple, with dark red-purple veins.

While they can grow to 17 inches, most pitcher plants range between 6 and 12 inches. Leaves develop each year from stems that emerge from underground rhizomes and remain evergreen, making them easy to find during winter months. Reproduction is typically by seed, with bees as the main pollinators, but may be accomplished by fragmentation of rhizomes.

Pitcher plants thrive in the acidic soils of savannas, flat woods near lakeshores, sphagnum moss and cedar bogs, and swamps—of which there are many in southern and central New Jersey. Spiders take advantage of the plant by spinning webs inside it to catch insects. Native Americans used the plant's root to treat tuberculosis and kidney ailments.

Another carnivorous plant to look for in moist-poor soils is the tiny sundew. It emits a sticky fluid that clings like dewdrops to catch and hold insects. Hairs press the victim down onto the surface of the blade, where it is then digested.

Turn Mill Lake, Lake Success, and Colliers Mill Lake
Colliers Mill (Ocean)

Remote and quiet, three lakes nestle into the landscape within Colliers Mill Wildlife Management Area. The surroundings are typical of the Pine Barrens pine and mixed-oak hardwood forests, with cedar, sweet gum, and red maple edging the water. Mountain laurel, sheep laurel, and the fragrant sweet pepperbush comprise most of the understory shrubs. The northern pine snake, whose range is primarily in and around South Carolina and Georgia, has small, disjunct colonies within the pinelands of New Jersey. Inhabiting only flat, sandy pine barrens, their secretive burrowing behavior eludes even the most experienced snake hunter. Pickerel, smallmouth bass, and sunfish live in the tea-colored waters typical of the Pine Barrens. Goldenrod flowers splash the landscape with yellow from late summer through fall, when they are joined by bouquets of wild blue asters.

Numerous coves edge Turn Mill Lake's 100 acres as you paddle to its southeastern end, where a few islands are tucked close to shore. The only drawback to the lake is that on some weekends local gun clubs use an established firing range for practice shooting. Though the range is not close, the sound echoes through the stillness. Should a gun club be present on the day you visit, you may want to drive out to Lake Success.

Because it is highly wash-boarded, the road to Lake Success seems much longer than its 3.0 miles—I call it the "kidney test track." Pitch pine, cedar, and sweet gum border the lake's 40 acres along with a number of beaches for informal picnics. Cedar swamps on its western end are ideal for bird watching. Numerous species of frogs, toads, and snakes relish this vast wilderness tract in the northern pinelands.

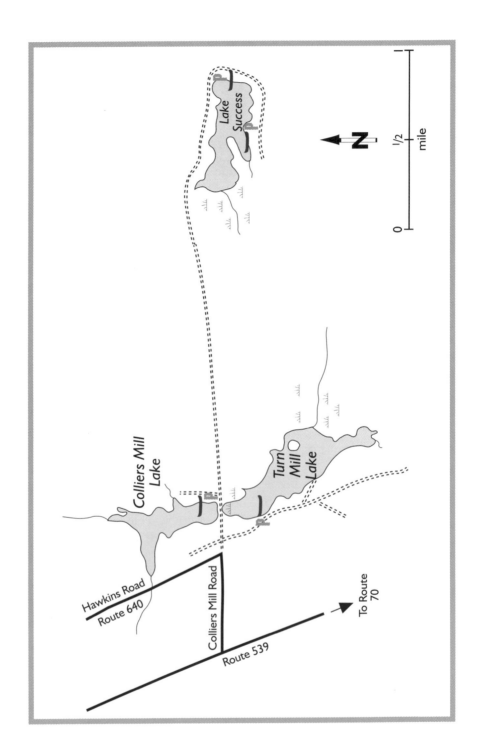

Colliers Mill Lake lies just off the main sand road near the entrance and, although it's used as a picnic spot in the summer, is never very crowded.

Getting there

From Route 70 near Whiting, drive 9.6 miles north on Route 539. Turn right onto Colliers Mill Road and drive 1.1 miles to the entrance of Colliers Mill Wildlife Management Area, which will be right in front of you. All roads are sandy and somewhat rutted. Parking is informal.

To Turn Mill Lake: From the entrance drive 100 feet and turn right (south) onto the sand road. Drive 0.2 mile to the launch site on your left. Parking is available in a small clearing on your right, about 40 feet down the road.

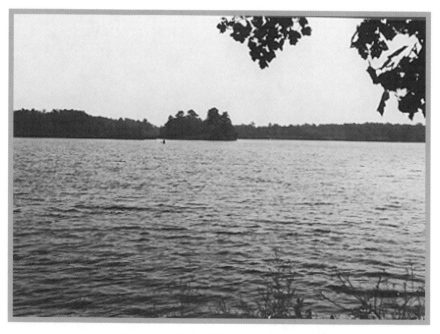

A canoeist approaches one of the islands on Turn Mill Lake.

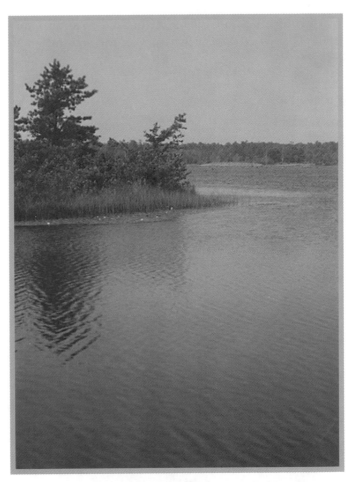

Cedar swamps on the northern end of Lake Success provide ample habitat for turtles, frogs, and songbirds.

To Colliers Mill Lake: From the entrance, drive straight ahead (east) 0.2 mile and turn left. Launch and informal parking are right there.

To Lake Success: From Colliers Mill Lake, continue east on the main road another 3.4 miles to the first launch area, which will be on your right. This is not the best launch site, as sugar-soft sand forces you to carry your boat about 75 feet, but the launch area is very pretty and makes a perfect informal picnic area under the shade of scrub pine trees. If you have four-wheel drive, you can drive about 50 feet closer for a shorter carry. The better launch site is another 0.2 mile around the lake, again on your right. Studded with pines, this also makes a nice informal picnic setting. New Jersey Division of Fish and Wildlife, Central Region (Assunpink WMA), 386 Clarksburg-Robbinsville Road, Robbinsville, NJ 08691; 609-259-2132.

Whitesbog Ponds
Whitesbog (Ocean)

If you love birding and butterflies, you'll love Whitesbog. Nature lovers from all over the state visit the exquisite bogs that were once part of a privately owned cranberry operation. Its history goes back to the mid-nineteenth century, when Colonel Fenwick purchased the land for experimental cranberry production. The farm soon became the largest cranberry producer in New Jersey, and in the late-nineteenth century the family began blueberry farming on the drier land around the bogs. Colonel Fenwick's granddaughter, Elizabeth, worked on the farm with Dr. Frederick Colville to cultivate the blueberries. Many of today's

White and yellow pond lilies carpet the launch site to Otter Pond.

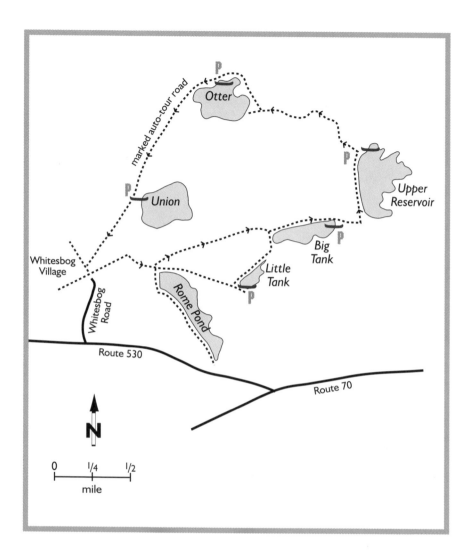

Otter

marked auto-tour road

P

P

Union

P

Upper Reservoir

Big Tank

Little Tank

P

P

Rome Pond

Whitesbog Village

Whitesbog Road

Route 530

Route 70

N

0   1/4   1/2
mile

blueberry strains in South Jersey originated from their venture. The state purchased the lands in the late 1960s with Green Acre funds and annexed the area to Lebanon State Forest. Projects funded by the New Jersey Division of Parks and Forestry and the Whitesbog Preservation Trust are restoring some of the original buildings in the tiny village.

Four attractive ponds and more than ten miles of trails can take a few days to explore if you really stop to observe the wildlife. Birds and

A painted turtle climbs atop a cedar stump to bask in the sun.

butterflies thrive in and around the bogs, where a rich source of berries, wildflowers, and fresh water provide them with an ideal habitat. Noted as a prime location to view the spring migration of neotropical songbirds, the New Jersey Audubon Society and various bird-watching groups sponsor bird-watching walks here year-round. Shallow pond waters and cedar stumps provide the perfect habitat for bog and painted turtles. Walking the open fields offers an opportunity to spot an Eastern milksnake, whose black-bordered, reddish-brown blotches stand out in striking contrast to its grayish-tan body.

During summer, nodding heads of orange and red milkweed throw dashes of brilliant color on open grasslands, along with accents of deep-blue loosestrife. In late summer, yellow goldenrod, blue aster, and soft purple joe-pye weed pick up the color accents. Whitesbog Village hosts a blueberry festival in July, where you can find blueberry pies, muffins, pancakes, and preserves.

Getting there

Getting there is easy; getting around inside can be challenging if you stray off the main road. All roads within the area are sand and parts of the roads have deep ruts, so drive slowly. From Route 70, drive 1.1 miles north on Route 530, turn right onto Whitesbog Road, and drive 0.3 mile to the village.

The map here has been greatly simplified. Roads shown are those marked for the auto-tour trail through the complex. Follow them. A more detailed map is available at the information billboard in the center of Whitesbog Village. New Jersey Division of Fish and Wildlife, Central Region (Assunpink WMA), 386 Clarksburg-Robbinsville Road, Robbinsville, NJ 08691; 609-259-2132.

Weequahic Lake
Newark (Union)

Weequahic Park is another gem in the midst of an urban area. An 80-acre lake, its miles of hiking and biking trails, soccer fields, and picnic areas transport you to a different world. The lake has been closed to boating for two years to allow dredging, cleaning, and water monitoring, but it is scheduled to re-open in the summer of 2001, when

Willow and beech trees border Weequahic Lake, noted for its huge carp.

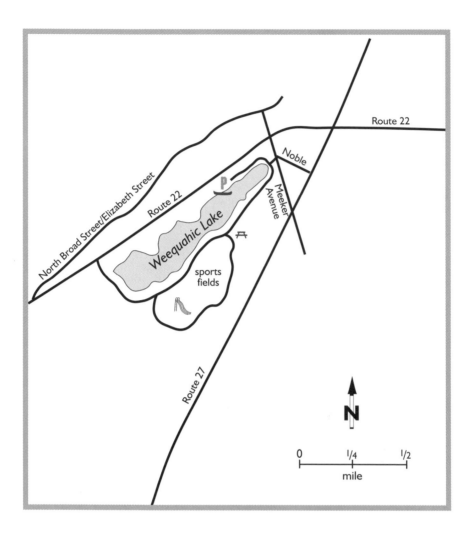

renovations to the boat launch area are complete. The deeply scalloped
south and west sides offer the best paddling, as huge trees hug the
shores beneath wooded hills. A local angler I talked with proudly
displayed the large carp he had caught earlier saying, "There's lots o'
big carp in these waters. Can catch one 'bout every day I come here."
Sports fields and larger picnic areas are located far enough away, so that
only muffled sounds reach the lake.

Getting there

From east and north of the park, drive Route 22 west to the Frelinguysen/Route 27 exit. Turn left at the end of the ramp onto Frelinguysen Avenue, drive 0.2 mile, and turn right onto Noble Street. Drive one block to the T, turn right onto Meeker Avenue, and drive for 200 feet to the park entrance on the left.

From south and west of the park, take Route 22 east to the Hillside Avenue/North Broad Street exit. Turn right at the end of the ramp and make an immediate left onto North Broad Street. Stay in the right-hand lane. North Broad Street becomes Elizabeth Street three blocks down, where you'll see the park on your right. Continue straight on Elizabeth Street for 0.6 mile (the end of the park) and turn right onto Meeker Avenue. The park entrance is about 200 feet ahead on your right. New Jersey Division of Fish and Wildlife, Central Region (Assunpink WMA), 386 Clarksburg-Robbinsville Road, Robbinsville, NJ 08691; 609-259-2132.

Southern New Jersey

Pine Barrens. The name not only describes the environment but is the formal name given to this vast area that covers more than two-thirds of the land in the southern half of New Jersey. Recognized on every U.S. governmental level for its ecological importance and enormous water resources, in 1983 the United Nations officially designated close to one million acres, about one-quarter of the state's total land area, the Pinelands National Reserve. The original Flemish settlers referred to this land as barren because traditional crops would not grow in the acidic conditions. These soils, however, provide a perfect environment

Approximate area covered by
the Pinelands National Reserve.

for blueberry and cranberry growth, making New Jersey one of the leading producers for both products. Due to these barren lands and the numerous state forests and Wildlife Management Areas acquired by the state over the past half century, southern New Jersey remains the least populated region in the state. To find out more about the Pine Barrens, contact Pinelands National Reserve, P.O. Box 7, 15 Springfield Road, New Lisbon, NJ 19106; 609-894-9342.

Enormous stands of Atlantic white cedar provided wood for a large shipbuilding industry in the mid-1900s. Shipbuilders Viking, Egg Harbor Yacht, and Ocean Yacht are still in existence today, though most of their boats are made of fiberglass. Behind the barrier islands rimming the Atlantic Ocean, vast expanses of tidal salt marshes create one of nature's most productive nursery grounds, offering nourishment and shelter for juvenile fish, crabs, and other inhabitants of coastal waters.

Batsto Lake
Pleasant Mills (Burlington)

Nestled in Wharton State Forest in the heart of the Pine Barrens along Route 542, Batsto Historical Village offers a look at eighteenth and nineteenth century living when the village boomed with more than 200 residents. A dam was built in 1765 along the Batsto River, creating the present-day lake and bogs, to provide power to operate a blast furnace for the production of iron—the first commercial operation at Batsto. Bog iron "ore" begins to form when vegetative matter decays and settles in soils containing high amounts of soluble iron. The ensuing chemical reaction brings the iron in solution to the surface, where it oxidizes upon contact with air. The heavier oxidized iron then settles to the bottom as a reddish-brown scum or sludge, cementing together bits of sand and gravel and then hardening to produce ironstone, or bog iron, in a process that takes about 30 years.

Surrounding forests provided the wood that was converted to charcoal to fuel the furnaces. Iron was used to make kitchenware items such as pots, stoves, and utensils, but the metal was in particular demand for the production of cannons and cannonballs during the French and Indian and Revolutionary Wars. In the mid-nineteenth century, large deposits of coal in Pennsylvania proved more efficient to burn than charcoal. The discovery of better iron ore deposits in the west and the depletion of local bog iron beds forced the collapse of most ironwork furnaces in New Jersey.

Furnaces such as that in Batsto were then used in the production of glass, even though there were already a number of glass factories in existence in southern New Jersey. The sand in the state's southern region is composed primarily of silica, the basic ingredient in glass, and if there's one thing South Jersey has it's sand—and lots of it! Supposedly, the towns of Green Bank and Crowleytown produced a green glass from which the original mason jars were made. Both of

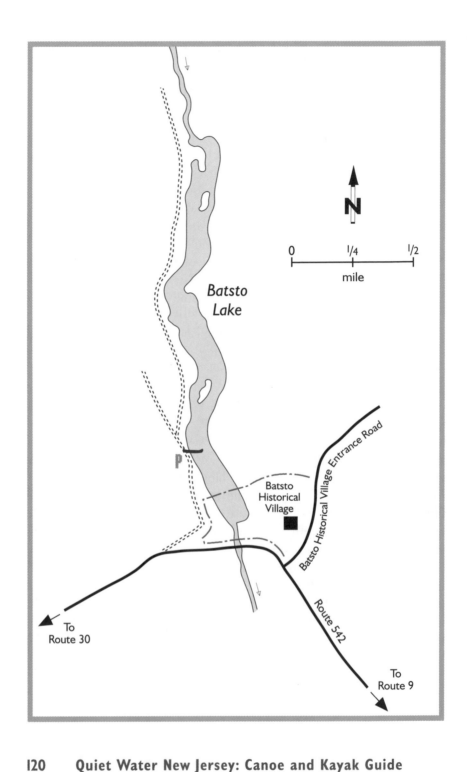

Batsto
Lake

N

0   1/4   1/2
mile

P

Batsto Historical Village Entrance Road

Batsto
Historical
Village

Route 542

To
Route 30

To
Route 9

these towns are located within 4.0 miles of Batsto Historical Village eastward along Route 542. A few remnants of old foundations on sandy back roads are all that remain of their furnace operations.

The launch site to Batsto Lake is on its southwestern end just outside the limits of Batsto Village. To the right of the launch will be a small dam and a few park buildings belonging to the village. You can paddle around there, but it is illegal to land on the property: signs are posted to that effect. To your left (north) it may look like the lake is very small and ends where the land juts out prominently, but paddle up the eastern edge and the larger portion of the lake will come into view. Two sandy beaches on the western shore of the northern end make great places to stop for lunch or just get out and stretch.

The first thing you may notice is the color of the water, a deep tea-color typical of the Pine Barrens. Natural tannins and acids leached from cedar trees, coupled with the naturally high iron content of surrounding soils, stain the water this deep reddish-brown. It may also leave a slight stain at the waterline on your boat, which is easily washed off. Lake depths generally average three to six feet, with slightly deeper waters where the river channel cuts through.

Around the lake you'll find a wide variety of dry upland and aquatic vegetation typical of the Pine Barrens. Oak and pine dominate the forest on the western and southern sides, along with a sprinkling of holly, tupelo, and sassafras. Red maple, swamp magnolia, sweet gum, and white cedar dominate in moist, low-lying areas. Swamp magnolias grace the landscape with large white blossoms that scent the air lightly from May through early July. The long, slender racemes of white flowers on sweet pepperbush release a refreshing fragrance detectable from 50 feet away. In fall, crimson leaves of red maple join the vivid yellow, orange, and red-rust of sweet gums to provide a delightful contrast to the deep green cedar and pine. Mountain and sheep laurel, huckleberry, wild blueberry, sweet pepperbush, and chokeberry fill the understory. A great treat while paddling late June through early August is to scout the shoreline for blueberry bushes—and there are plenty of them. Wild blueberries are smaller than their cultivated counterparts, but much sweeter. Along the banks in late summer and fall, look for the matlike growth of wild cranberries, whose yellow-green berries start turning bright red in late September.

The northern section of the lake, particularly on the western side, becomes a shallow, swamplike environment. Here you want to paddle slowly or sit quietly, waiting for the bird life to come to you. Cedar becomes more prominent, requiring moist or sodden soils. Fragrant white water lilies and yellow pond lilies carpet the lake's surface in its coves, and its blue-purple spikes of flowers poke up from the arrow-shaped leaves of the pickerelweed.

Osprey and turkey vultures frequent the northern half of the lake, along with grackles, fish crows, and various species of duck, the latter being more prominent in late summer and fall. If you're lucky, you'll get to see a bald eagle that has frequented the area for years. One of these days, I'm going to find its nest. Great blue herons search the shallows for fish, while blue jays shriek through the trees. Warblers, swifts (I love them—they eat mosquitoes), gray catbird, goldfinch, cardinal,

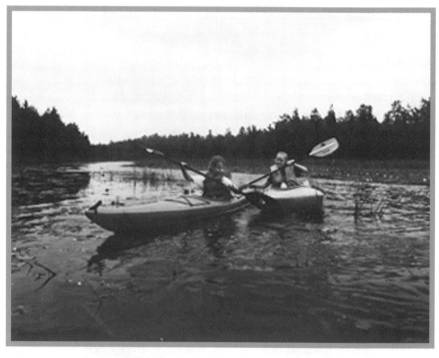

These two young friends have just completed their first kayaking experience. I'd say they're hooked.

rufous-sided towhee, woodpeckers, eastern phoebe, and eastern kingbird are among the most frequently observed birds. Rufous-sided towhees are the most characteristic bird of upland pine barrens.

An abundant population of painted turtles, some of them quite large, sun themselves on fallen limbs and cedar stumps. Snapping turtles are common but rarely seen since they spend most of their time underwater. A number of beaver huts dot the length of Batsto River. The southernmost one can be seen from the north end of the lake and usually has three or four large turtles hanging around on the firm sand near the water's edge.

Due to the high acidity and iron content of the water and its low nutrient level, fish and amphibian diversity is limited. Chain and redfin pickerel and yellow and brown bullheads (catfish) are about the only species fished for in this lake. The small blackbanded sunfish, with its striking black and white bands and angular body shape, is the most characteristic species of the Pine Barrens.

If you would like to get in a little hiking, the sandy road at the launch site continues north, paralleling the lake and river. Local livery services use it to drop paddlers off a few miles up the Batsto River. On a larger scale, the Batona Trail starts at Batsto Historical Village and travels northeast for 25 miles to Lebanon State Forest. You can hike all or part of this trail, which winds through dry upland pinelands, lowland swamps, and cranberry bogs. Be prepared for ticks while hiking, and check yourself frequently.

During summer, Batsto Historical Village hosts an antique car show, blueberry and cranberry festivals, and other family events, some of which include candle making, ironworking, and other crafts of the bygone era. Pony rides and other activities for children are usually included. There is no camping around the lake, but there are several state-run campgrounds inside Wharton State Forest, plus a few private campgrounds in the vicinity. Stop in at the Batsto park office located near Mile Marker 9 on Route 542 for camping information and a calendar of events. Camping is also available at Bel Haven Lake Resort Campground, 1213 Route 542, Green Bank, NJ 08215; 609-965-2827.

Getting There

Access to the lake is from a sand road off Route 542 near Mile Marker 8 (but there is no Mile Marker 8 post) at the western end of Batsto Historical Village, where the split-rail fence surrounding the village turns back into the woods.

From Route 30, drive east 6.2 miles on Route 542 to where the road bends sharply to the right (east). At that bend, you will see the wood split-rail fence that surrounds the historical village. Drive into the sandy clearing to the left of the fence and follow the sand road 0.3 mile to the launch site. The road parallels the wood fence for about half of the drive. Parking space for about 12 vehicles is next to the sandy ramp.

From Route 206 the turnoff to Batsto is exactly at Mile Marker 3. Turn left (you can't go right) onto Route 613 and proceed 2.4 miles to the first intersection. Turn left (a small brown Batsto sign is at the intersection), drive 0.3 mile to the T, and turn left onto Route 693. Hammonton airport will be immediately on your left (don't blink or you'll miss it). Continue straight (but it's a crooked road) for 5.7 miles to the T; turn left onto Route 542 east and continue 3.9 miles to the sand entrance road.

From northbound Garden State Parkway, take Exit 50 onto north Route 9; Route 542 west intersects 1.3 miles up the road—careful, this is a hairpin turn. Turn left onto Route 542 and drive 7.2 miles to the sand entrance road on the right. You will pass the Batsto Historical Village visitor center on the right about 0.6 mile before the boat access road.

From southbound Garden State Parkway, take Exit 52 and turn left at the end of the ramp onto East Greenbush. Drive 3.0 miles to the T. Turn right (south) onto Route 9 and drive 2.4 miles to its junction with Route 542 west (on the right). Near Mile Marker 9 on Route 542, the entrance road to the Batsto Historical Village visitor center will be on the right. Drive another 0.6 mile to the sand road on the right. Wharton State Forest, 4110 Nesco Road, Hammonton, NJ 08037; 609-561-0024.

Atsion Lake
Shamong (Burlington)

One of the larger lakes within the 110,000-acre Wharton State Forest, Atsion Lake (pronounced *AT-zon* by locals) is the only one that provides on-site camping facilities, many of which are lakeside. White water lilies carpet the shallower western end, where the headwaters of the Mullica River, the largest waterway in the Pine Barrens, feed into the lake.

Thick pine and oak woods surround the lake, with a few stands of Phragmites along shallower shores. Red maple, hickory, and birch trees poke their branches between dark green pine and cedar at the water's

Cedar and sweet gum line the shores of Atsion Lake.

edge, creating a colorful contrast in fall. Most of the lake is fairly deep by coastal plain standards, with some spots reaching depths of 15 feet or more.

Nine lakeside log cabins, each offering a private car-top launch, are available on the northeastern end of the lake, and a large campground on the northwestern end offers a few on-water sites. Public boat launch, playgrounds, showers, swimming beach, nature trails, and picnic facilities are provided at the recreation area on the south side of the lake.

Getting there

From Route 30 drive north 7.3 miles on Route 206 and turn left into the recreation area. The boat ramp is on the far side of the parking lot. The park office is 0.3 mile north on the east (right) side of the road.

From Route 70, drive south 10.2 miles on Route 206, turn right into the entrance, and proceed as above. Wharton State Forest/Atsion Office, 744 Route 206, Shamong, NJ 08088; 609-268-0444.

Pine Barrens Tree Frog
(Hyla andersonii)

Occurring nowhere else in New Jersey, the chorus of the Pine Barrens tree frog fills the air on late spring evenings during breeding season. They inhabit shallow pools in sphagnum bogs, backwater and slow-moving streams, cranberry bogs, and cedar swamps. Requiring acidic environments, the tree frog's habitat is susceptible to any human infringement that raises the pH level or decreases the water table. Considered a threatened species, preservation of the tree frog's specific wetland habitat is crucial for survival. Only a few other disjunct populations have been found in the acidic bogs of the Carolinas, Georgia, and western Florida.

Lavender stripes bordered in white create a striking contrast to the tree frog's emerald-green inch-and-a-half long, body. Bright yellow and orange conceals the surfaces of its legs. As indicative of tree frogs, its long, webbed toes end in adhesive discs that enable it to cling to twigs and bark. Insects and other invertebrates found in moist environments constitute its main diet. Males produce a nasally *quonk-quonk-quonk* sound through vocal sacks that inflate like a balloon. Though heard in vast numbers, the tree frog is difficult to find unless you patiently follow the call to its source. Breeding and egg-laying take place in May and June, with its larvae metamorphosing into adults by July to early August. Due to their secretive lives, little is known about the tree frog's behavior outside the breeding season.

Mannington Meadows
Pennsville (Salem)

Neither a lake nor a bay, Mannington Meadows' vast expanse of brackish waters can fill days of paddling enjoyment for the nature lover. Situated close to the Delaware River, its waters are slightly tidal. A torturous network of narrow channels at the mouth of the Salem River snakes its way around tiny islands and buffers most of the tidal current effect. You'll notice as the day wears on a slightly higher or lower waterline along the shores. With more than 3,000 acres in this low-lying coastal plain, you will probably need to push yourself off a sandbar or two when the tide is out, particularly in the narrower side channels. Deeper waters lie along the eastern shoreline, where the Salem River has cut a deep channel. Supawna Meadows National Wildlife Refuge adjoins Mannington Meadows along the latter's southwestern flank. The refuge provides wintering and migrating waterfowl with an important feeding and resting area.

Egrets, herons, shorebirds, pintails, black ducks, cormorants, woodcocks, songbirds, and a plethora of other bird species are common visitors. Osprey and wood ducks that nest at the nearby refuge come to Mannington Meadows often to hunt. Frogs, turtles, and muskrats are abundant along the shallower eastern shores, where they live among wide fields of water lilies and marsh grasses. Look for the diamondback terrapin, one of the few turtles that inhabits brackish waters on a consistent basis.

The launch is located along a channel in the northwestern end of the meadows. Paddle right to enter the meadows proper, or paddle left into channels where you're likely to see muskrats, or at least evidence that they live here.

To
I-295
and
NJ Turnpike

N

0   ¹/₂   1
mile

East Pittsfield

Hook Road

Route 551

Pointers Auburn Road

Route 540

Route 49

Mannington
Meadows

Route 49

Route 45

SUPAWNA MEADOWS
NATIONAL WILDLIFE
REFUGE

Looking through one of the many coves in the brackish marshlands of Mannington Meadows.

Getting there

From Route 49 on the southeast end of Pennsville, drive north on Route 551 (Hook Road) 2.0 miles. Turn right onto East Pittsfield Street and drive 0.7 mile to the boat launch and parking at the end of the road.

From the north, take I-295 or the New Jersey Turnpike south. Both highways come together for a short span right before the Delaware Memorial Bridge. Follow signs for the Pennsville/Salem/ "last exit before toll" exit ramp. Drive 0.3 mile and turn left, following

the signs for "Hook Road/40 East to Tpk. and Atlantic City Expy."
Drive 0.5 mile, following the signs to Hook Road. The road will bend
to the right and put you onto Hook Road. Drive 1.2 miles, turn left
onto East Pittsfield, and continue 0.8 mile to the launch—the blacktop
will end about halfway to the end. Parking is informal.

For information about nearby Supawna Meadows National
Wildlife Refuge, contact them at 229 Lighthouse Road, Salem, NJ
08079; 609-935-1487.

Stafford Forge Ponds
Stafford Forge (Ocean)

Stafford Forge Wildlife Management Area is home to three ponds, originally cranberry bogs, where countless herons, egrets, ducks, and other water birds inhabit the rich environment. Atlantic white cedar, sweet gum, and red maple dominate the scenery near the water, along with an occasional plush stand of Phragmites and cattails. Typical pine barren forests of mixed-oak and pitch pine fill the surrounding woods for miles. If you want solitude, this is it. Electric outboards are permitted, though I've never seen one, and hunting is allowed during specific seasons.

Listen for the telltale *eep, eep* of osprey that frequently fish these waters, especially in pond #1. If you do spot an osprey, keep an eye on it awhile—seeing one plunge into the water and come out with a fish in its talons is a rewarding experience. Great blue herons, great egrets, and mallards are the more common water birds here, while blue jays, warblers, and grackles regularly inhabit the woods. Small coves created by inlet streams dot the southern and northern shores of pond #3, the largest and deepest of the Stafford Forge ponds.

Late summer and early fall are the prettiest months to visit. Fluffy Phragmite heads laden with seed shimmer silvery-beige against a background of dark green cedar. Here and there, swamp-loving cardinal flowers add stokes of vibrant red, and water grasses turn a deep gold to rust. Mulberry bushes become deep scarlet and sweet gum trees splash vibrant yellow, orange, and red around the ponds. Be aware that in an extreme drought year, the normally shallow three- to five-foot deep waters can become nothing more than giant puddles.

Camping is available at Sea Pirate Campground located on the east side of Route 9, 5.0 miles south of Route 72. Contact them at P.O. Box 271, West Creek, NJ 08092; 609-296-7400.

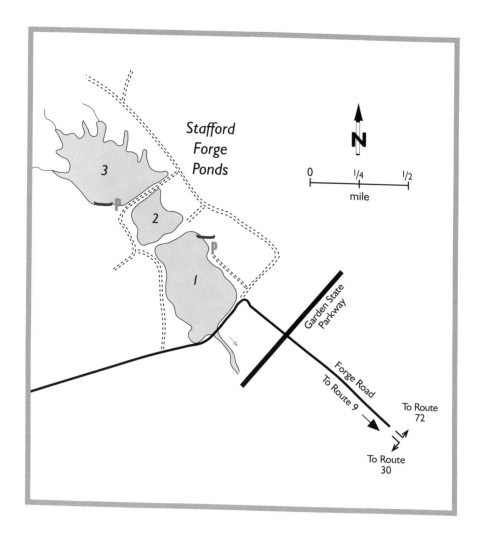

Getting there

From Route 72, drive south 3.7 miles on Route 9 and turn right onto Forge Road (there will be a sign for Stafford Forge Wildlife Management Area). Drive 1.9 miles and turn right onto the sand entrance road. *Caution!* Watch for what locals call "sugar sand,"—a very soft sand known to swallow even tow trucks whole. Only a few small spots are on the main roads, but they are prevalent on other back roads, should you go exploring.

**Pitch pine and oak stand behind cedar in
the northernmost pond.**

Pond #1: From the entrance, make an immediate left and drive 0.3
mile to the end. Put in anywhere on the sandy tip. Parking is informal.

Ponds #2 and #3: From the entrance, stay to your right and follow
the road around for 0.6 mile, turn left, and drive 0.4 mile to the other
end of the sand dike. As you pass over the dike, pond #3 will be on your
right, pond #2 on your left. A hard-sand launch for pond #3, the largest
and deepest of the ponds, will be on your right at the end of the dike.
Parking is informal. Pond #2 is accessed by turning left at the end of the
dike—drive 0.2 mile and launch from the sandy ramp. New Jersey
Division of Fish and Wildlife, Southern Region, (Winslow WMA),
229 Blue Anchor Road, Sicklerville, NJ 08081; 856-629-0090.

Newton Lake and Cooper River Park Lake
Collingswood (Camden)

Newton Lake is another attractive lake in the midst of a highly populated area. A rim of a municipal park of the same name surrounds the 40-acre lake. Walking paths weave their way around trees along the landscaped swath of land dotted with lakeside benches and small gardens. Long and narrow, the lake's serpentine shape provides a long, relaxing paddle. Parking is curbside, parallel to the road by the lake. If you can park at the launch site, you'll only have a 40-foot portage, but expect a longer carry if you visit on a crowded day and need to park farther away.

Over the years the city has cleaned up its waters and created a lovely park along a 2.5-mile stretch of the Cooper River where it widens to a few hundred yards—enough to call it a lake at least by South Jersey standards. For those who live in the densely populated Camden area and need a place close to home, this section of the river landscaped with trees, shrubs, and small garden areas provides the perfect refuge. The best paddling is on the eastern end, where the shores become more wooded and you're farther from bustling traffic. Biking and hiking trails snake their way along both shores, and portable toilets are conveniently located all along the grounds.

One launch spot on the east end of the north shore has a small pagoda set slightly back from the water's edge, creating an attractive setting. The park is closed from midnight until 6:00 A.M., leaving plenty of time for a moonlight paddle. A large concrete boat ramp with ample parking is available on the south shore.

pagoda

North Park Drive

Cuthbert Boulevard

Cooper River Park Lake

South Park Drive

Coleford Street

Collins Road

Newton Lake

Newton Park Drive

White Horse Pike

Route 30

Route 168

Newton Avenue

N

0   1/4   1/2
mile

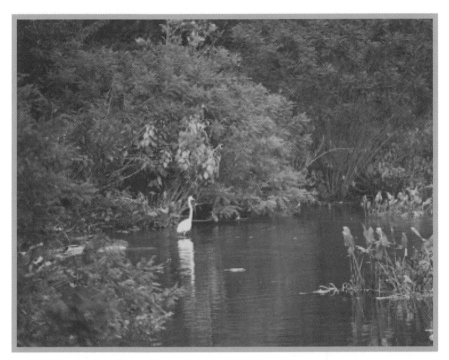

A great egret walks along the shallow edges of Newton Lake between rafts of pickerelweed.

Getting there

To Cooper River Park Lake: From the Routes 130/30 circle, drive north 0.4 mile on Route 130, turn right onto South Park Drive, and continue 0.9 mile to the boat launch and parking area on your left. An additional car-top launch can be found 1.0 mile down South Park Drive just after crossing Cuthbert Boulevard. Park your car and carry your boat about 20 feet to the grassy bank.

To launch from the north shore at the pagoda, drive north 0.6 mile on Route 130 from the Routes 130/30 circle. Turn right onto North Park Drive and drive 2.3 miles, crossing Cuthbert Boulevard along the way.

To Newton Lake: From the Routes 130/30 circle, drive east 0.7 mile on Route 30, turn left onto Newton Park Drive (it's Newton Avenue on the right), and drive 0.45 mile to Coleford Street. A small stone dock is on the lake directly across from Coleford Street. Park on Newton Park Drive on the lake side as close as possible to Coleford Street. New Jersey Division of Fish and Wildlife, Southern Region, (Winslow WMA), 229 Blue Anchor Road, Sicklerville NJ 08081; 856-629-0090.

Shaw's Mill Pond
Newport (Cumberland)

Fortesque, a town on the Delaware Bay known throughout most of South Jersey for its fantastic crabbing industry, lies only a short distance from Shaw's Mill Pond. It's worth a trip to the little village after paddling Shaw's Mill Pond, where you will enjoy exploring the numerous inlets and coves in this isolated setting surrounded by woods. Bass,

Plenty of coves and inlets to explore at Shaw's Mill Pond, along with hiking trails through a protected wildlife habitat.

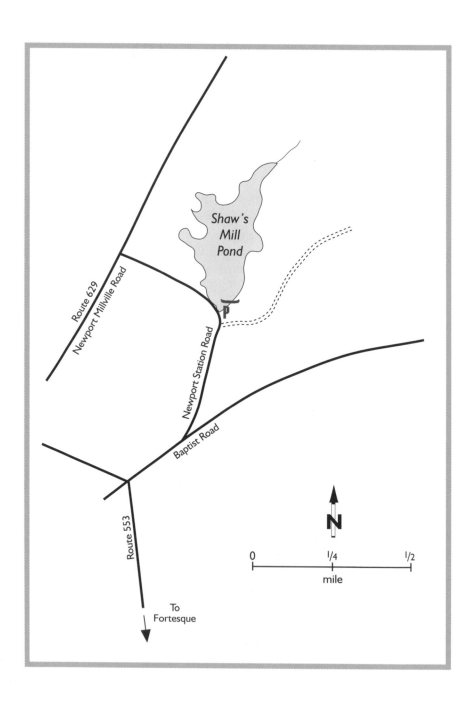

pickerel, and perch swim beneath the quiet waters. Miles of hiking trails on the east side of the pond wind through woods set aside to protect wildlife habitat; no vehicles are permitted on roads through the area. Gas motors are prohibited on the pond.

Getting there

From Route 610, drive south 2.7 miles on Route 553 (Main Street), turn left on Baptist Road, and drive 0.5 mile. Bear left at the fork—this is Newport Station Road, but there is no sign—drive 0.4 mile to the pond. The road turns left here, but you want to drive to the right onto the sand parking area and launch, both of which are informal. To reach another access, get back on the road and drive another 0.1 mile, passing over the creek bridge. Turn right after the bridge onto the sand area. New Jersey Division of Fish and Wildlife, Southern Region, (Winslow WMA), 229 Blue Anchor Road, Sicklerville, NJ 08081; 856-629-0090.

Manahawkin Impoundment and Bridge to Nowhere
Manahawkin (Ocean)

So where does the Bridge to Nowhere go? Just where its name implies; hence the funky moniker locals gave this part of Barnegat National Wildlife Refuge. Situated far from inlets where tidal currents have minimal effect, this is an excellent spot to explore the salt marshes and back waters of Barnegat Bay. From the launch next to the bridge, paddle to your right (south) down the meandering channel leading to the bay. Once you exit the channels it would be wise to turn around, get your bearings, and note landmark positions before paddling in the open

Egrets, herons, and swans are frequent visitors to the impoundment.

Barnegat Bay

To Barnegat Bay

Cedar Creek

Bridge to Nowhere

Manahawkin Impoundment

Route 72

Bay Avenue

Hillard Boulevard

Stafford Road

Route 9

N

0   ½   mile

Tidal saltwater marshes on the mainland side of Barnegat Bay provide a refuge for wading and shorebirds.

waters. Since the marsh area sticks out prominently, it's easy to find your way back, but you'll have better piece of mind if you take that extra step on your first few trips here. You also can turn left from the launch into a maze of channels if you feel adventurous and have a good sense of direction.

Snowy and great egrets are abundant in the shallow waters along the banks, along with an occasional great blue heron. Narrow side channels lead into the wider main channel along the way; check them out when you pass, as sandpipers and egrets often prefer these more secluded waters.

Tall reeds and a smattering of bayberry bushes rim the shores around Manahawkin Impoundment. Marsh wrens, tough birds to spot, fill the air with their nervous, high-pitched twitter from inside dense Phragmites stands. Between the reeds and the oak-dominated lowland woods behind them, cedar and red maple take hold on the moist middle ground. The impoundment is small, but it makes a delightful side trip on the way to the Bridge to Nowhere. Swans and ducks swim on the waters, and cedar waxwings usually can be spotted on the dense clusters of cedar on the far end.

Getting there

From Route 72, drive north 0.1 mile on Route 9 to the Bay Avenue traffic light. One hundred feet north of Bay Avenue, turn right onto Stafford Road and drive 2.0 miles to Hillard Boulevard. From there, Stafford Road continues straight as a rough washboard sand road—go slow. Continue another 1.5 miles; the small launch to the impoundment will be on the right. The road widens slightly here for parking, which is casual. Park parallel to the road and close to roadside vegetation so other cars can pass easily.

To the Bridge to Nowhere: Continue down Stafford Road another 0.6 mile to the end. A wooden bridge spans the creek. Launch from the left side of the bridge, where you'll see a narrow path leading to the creek. New Jersey Division of Fish and Wildlife, Southern Region, (Winslow WMA), 229 Blue Anchor Road, Sicklerville, NJ 08081; 856-629-0090.

Snowy Egret
(Egreta thula)

At first glance, the snowy egret might be confused with the great egret, another member of the family *Ardeidae* with stark white feathers, black legs, and a long, slender neck. But the great egret, in addition to being much larger, sports a yellow beak and black toes; the snowy egret has a black beak and yellow toes. Avid birders refer to snowy egrets as "snegs" and great egrets as "gregs." Members of *Ardeidae* have several things in common: long necks that fold into an S shape in flight, spearlike bills, and legs that trail when flying. Adult snowy egrets have shaggy heads, necks, and back plumes that are clearly visible when not in flight—almost as if they forgot to comb their hair.

Snowy egrets typically frequent wetland environments such as salt marshes, and brackish marshes, ponds, and swamps within the coastal plain. While it is not unusual to spot a solitary egret, they are more often found in small colonies, foraging for food. Occasionally they maintain their own separate feeding territory. If you hear a lot of low croaking and see some feathers rustling, chances are that a snowy egret felt its territory had been infringed upon.

Commensal feeding, where one species gives a feeding advantage to another, is prevalent among snowy egrets and ibis and other herons. Most egrets and herons forage in a "stalk and strike" method. While they may initially stalk, snowy egrets shuffle their feet in a flurry to stir up aquatic invertebrates, a favorite prey. In the process, many creatures are sent scurrying and made available to other birds foraging within a few feet. Small fish, reptiles, and insects are also hunted in lesser quantities.

The long nuptial head plumes that snowy egrets develop during breeding season almost caused their demise in the late nineteenth and early twentieth centuries, when large colonies of snowy, red, and great egrets were killed for their ornamental breeding plumes that were used to make ladies' hats. The plumes also were highly sought after as ornaments in Asian ceremonial dress. In 1901 the National Audubon Society sponsored a law prohibiting the killing of any bird except game birds. In the Everglades, where large breeding colonies existed, a labyrinth of narrow channels filled with mosquitoes and alligators made it impossible to patrol. As a result, plume hunters continued to make money as species counts dwindled. In 1903 plumes sold for $32 an ounce, slightly more than the price of gold at the time!

East Creek Pond and Lake Nummy
Woodbine (Cape May)

Miles and miles of hiking trails meander through more than 15,000 acres of upland oak and pine forests, hardwood forests, Atlantic white cedar swamps, and bogs within Belleplain State Forest. Situated on the outskirts of Pine Barren lands, the better soil conditions here allow for a wider variety of trees and shrubs, including hickory, beech, and ash. Two bodies of water, East Creek Pond and Lake Nummy, lie completely within the park's boundaries. The smaller of the two, Lake Nummy, centers around the park's campground, swimming beach, and recreational area on the east and south shores and becomes quite crowded in summer. Part of the north end of the lake ducks under a footpath bridge, making a quaint little paddle for novices or parents taking their children out for the first time.

A group cabin sits off a small county road near the short southern end of East Creek Pond. Numerous coves and inlets house large populations of painted and bog turtles, which bask in the sun on logs and cedar stumps. In summer, sweet pepperbush develops racemes of white flowers, which fill the air with a sweet aroma detectable for over 50 feet. For a sweet snack in July and August, look for blueberry bushes that peek out along the edge of the lake. Arrow weed, pickerelweed, and water lilies along the shallower shores provide a protective environment for the young pickerel, smallmouth bass, sunfish, and crappie found in the lake.

Tent and trailer campsites are available, but only one site, a group cabin at East Creek Pond, is on the water. Yurts, a type of circular tent with wood floors, a deck, and a Plexiglas skylight, are also available for rent. No gas motors are permitted on the lake.

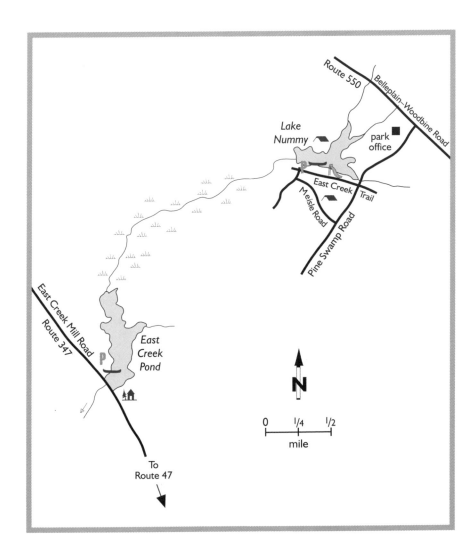

Getting there

To Lake Nummy and the visitor center: From Route 47 on the south side of Woodbine, drive north 3.1 miles on Route 557, turn left (west) onto Route 550, and drive 1.4 miles to the park entrance on your left. The visitor center will be on your right about 100 feet inside the park. Continue past the visitor center 0.35 mile, turn right onto Meisle Road, and drive 0.4 mile to the dock at Lake Nummy.

Two friends enjoy a lazy afternoon of paddling along the coves in East Creek Pond.

To East Creek Pond: From Route 557, drive north 0.7 mile on Route 47. The road forks here, with Route 47 going to the left and Route 347 to the right. Take the right fork onto Route 347 and drive 2.0 miles. Turn right into the boat ramp area on your right at the end of the guardrail. Belleplain State Forest, County Route 550, P.O. Box 450, Woodbine, NJ 08270; 609-861-2404.

Edwin B. Forsythe National Wildlife Refuge
Smithville (Atlantic)

This is one of those coastal bay areas I could not help but include because of its prodigious bird species, which can be observed year-round. Edwin B. Forsythe National Wildlife Refuge is one of the major stopovers along the Atlantic flyway for migratory birds. You will paddle out through the salt marshes and onto the backside of Great Bay. Spring and fall migrations bring large numbers of shorebirds, waterfowl, and wading birds to rest and feed before continuing their journey. Some remain for the entire summer. Diamondback terrapins, with their decorative concentric whorls, are found frequently in and around the marshes. Look skyward for bald eagles, osprey, peregrine falcons, and hawks.

Mid-May to early June, when migrating birds feast on horseshoe crab eggs in the Chesapeake and Delaware Bay estuaries, this refuge provides their next major stopover. One of my favorite early-summer migratory species is the Arctic tern—travelers from South America that stop here for a few weeks prior to continuing their journey to the Arctic. That's a total distance of 10,000 miles or more! In mid-October the sky is filled with large flocks of snow geese—large white birds with black-tipped wings. In winter black ducks, Atlantic brants, and Canada geese dominate the ponds.

On the nearby barrier islands, beaches and dunes provide nesting habitat for piping plovers, black skimmers, and least terns. Watch for posted signs if you decide to explore these islands; a few are primary nesting sites for the piping plover and off-limits during nesting season.

For the quickest trip to the refuge, paddle south (right) from the launch area. It's only about a 3.0-mile paddle to Hammock Cove on the north side of the refuge. You will probably see a car or two driving down the north dike of the refuge.

For a longer, more scenic trip, paddle north (left) from the launch area for about 1.0 mile to the bay. Once you're about 200 feet out into the bay take notice of the entrance to the creek you just exited and any visuals, such as channel markers and lights buoys. Never rely on inland coastal charts as a good storm can destroy or move markers. Take notice of where markers are today. Paddle south (right) around the salt marsh peninsula and into Hammock Cove, a distance of about 6.0 miles.

The drive-through part of the refuge can be reached by traveling south about 7.6 miles on Route 9 from Smithville to Oceanville. A large refuge sign on Route 9 directs you to the entrance. Open from dawn until dusk, the 8.0-mile vehicle loop takes you past upland fields and woodlands, coastal salt meadows and marshes, open bays, and channels. Two observation towers are located along the drive, the second of which is closest to the large, human-made peregrine nesting house. The visitor center, open 8:00 A.M. to 4:00 P.M. weekdays and weekends, displays numerous wildlife exhibits. Two short nature trails are located adjacent to the center—bring lots of mosquito repellent July through September. A small entrance fee is charged to enter the drive loop. Edwin B. Forsythe National Wildlife Refuge, Box 72, Oceanville, NJ 08231; 609-652-1665. Camping is available at Evergreen Woods Lakefront Resort on Moss Mill Road. Contact them at Box 197, Pomoa, NJ 08240; 609-652-1577.

Getting there

Scott's Landing boat ramp is located east of Smithville on Route 9. From the south: From Route 30, drive north 3.2 miles on Route 9, turn right (east) onto Route 561 (Moss Mill Road), and drive 1.5 miles. The

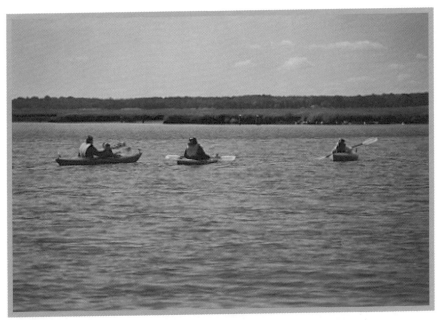

A family of kayakers paddle slowly near a flock of egrets.

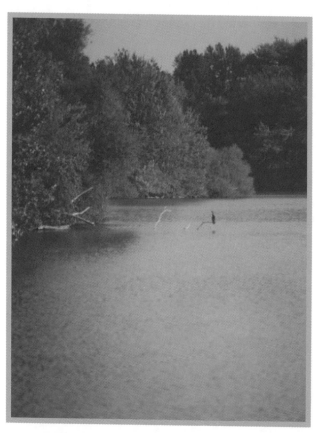

Cormorants swim underwater to catch their prey. Unlike ducks, their feathers are not water-proof so they must "dry out" occasionally.

road turns to the left here. Drive around the bend and take the next right, about 100 feet away. Follow that road 0.4 mile. The parking area will be on your left; the concrete boat ramp will be about 100 feet straight ahead.

From the north: Take Garden State Parkway Exit 48, which puts you onto Route 9 south. Drive 6.7 miles and turn left onto Route 561. Continue as above.

Camping is available at Evergreen Woods Lakefront Resort on Moss Mill Road. Contact them at Box 197, Pomoa, NJ 08240; 609-652-1577.

Union Lake
Millville (Cumberland)

Located in the southeast corner of Cumberland County on the western outskirts of Millville, Union Lake was created by the damming of the Maurice and Mill Rivers. This oblong lake covers 898 acres and is 4.0 miles long and 1.2 miles at its widest point. The state acquired the lake in the early 1990s and it is now a Fish and Wildlife Management Area. As at many other waterways in the state, Native American artifacts have been found here. The Vineland Historical and Antiquarian Society, at Seventh and Elmer Streets in Vineland, display many of the artifacts uncovered over the years.

While at Union Lake, keep your eyes sharp and you may find a real treasure. If you do find an artifact, take notes on its location as best you can before notifying the historical society. Don't move or remove the item, since archaeologists reconstruct the history of an area based on the exact location of various artifacts. Because this is state-owned property, keeping artifacts is illegal.

Pollution in the form of various chemicals, by-products from a paint production company in North Vineland, once plagued this waterway all the way to the Delaware Bay. Dumping stopped in the early 1980s largely due to pressure from surrounding communities and local environmental groups. With the river and lake cleaned up, you'll find not only some of the best fishing in southeastern New Jersey but also some of its cleanest and clearest waters for swimming and paddling. Consider a moonlight paddle here, when the full moon peeks through treetops before spraying a radiant glow across the water.

Bottom sediment consists primarily of tan sand, mud, and some gravel, except near the launch site around the dam, where it is shored up with trucked-in rocks. The average lake depth is 14 feet, with deeper pockets to 30 feet near the dam. Most coves have shallow margins, which are only two to four feet deep, perfect for a refreshing swim.

Close to shore, you'll find aquatic grasses piercing the water's surface between water lily pads. In recent years, tires and Christmas trees have been used to create artificial habitats. This effort provides key places for juvenile fish to hide from larger predators, thereby helping to increase fish populations. Numerous islands, coves, and peninsulas are found on the lake's western and northern areas.

Three islands, within 1.0 mile of the put-in off its southwest shore, each have one or two landing sites with small clearings for a picnic lunch and short walking trails to stretch your legs. The largest of these islands is Rattlesnake Island, named for the reptile once found in abundance there. Never fear though, rattlesnakes have not been seen on the island for at least eight years. Largemouth bass, colorful sunfish,

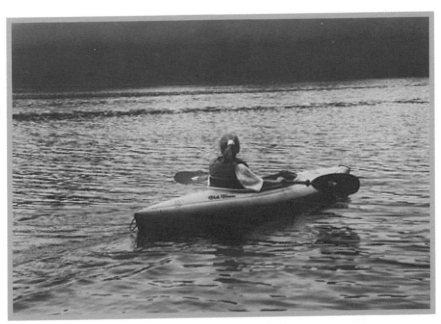

A young paddler in a moment of quiet contemplation at the end of a day.

catfish, pickerel, and yellow perch are caught by local anglers under the watchful eye of osprey, which nest along the lake's western shore.

The lake is also stocked with a hybrid fish, a cross between a striped bass and largemouth bass. Osprey and numerous species of ducks and geese frequent the lake. On a few occasions I've even seen a bald eagle scouting the clear water. Watch carefully and you might spot wood ducks or hooded merganser, particularly in the coves. At dawn you're likely to see whitetailed deer and raccoons sauntering along the shore. Short cliffs, about 0.75 mile down from the landing, host a few kingfisher nest holes. Look for their cavities about two feet above the waterline.

Sandy hiking trails meander along the western and northern lakeshores. Half of the eastern lakefront is residential, but there are some hiking trails along the northeast shore. The trails lead you through an oak and scrub pine forest with lowbush blueberry and sheep laurel dominating the understory. Closer to the water, you'll find red maple, birch, swamp magnolia, cedar, and mountain laurel. In late spring and early summer, dainty, pale pink mountain laurel and white sheep laurel blossoms sprinkle the landscape like pixie dust against a background of dark green cedar and evergreen laurel leaves. Early summer brings the sweet scent of swamp magnolias drifting across the landscape as their large white blossoms unfold.

While outboards are permitted, there is a ten-horsepower limit. Most outboard traffic I have encountered, and there isn't much, has been on the deeper, southeastern end of the lake close to the dam. The best and least crowded paddling is along the lake's western and northern shores where you can meander around islands and quiet coves.

Getting there

From Route 55 near Millville, take Exit 29 (Sherman Avenue) and turn west onto Sherman Avenue. Drive 2.5 miles, turn left onto Route 608 (Carmel Avenue), and drive 3.4 miles to Union Lake Wildlife Management Area on the left. Drive 0.2 mile to the parking area and concrete ramp. Portable toilets are available Memorial Day through Labor Day. For a woodsier launch, drive to the far end of the parking lot, where a wide trail leads to a small, sandy area about 50 feet from the parking lot.

If you come by way of Route 49 (Main Street), Carmel Avenue veers off Route 49 about 1.2 miles west of Route 47. Drive 2.0 miles on Carmel Avenue to the lake entrance on the right. New Jersey Division of Fish and Wildlife, Southern Region, (Winslow WMA), 229 Blue Anchor Road, Sicklerville, NJ 08081; 856-629-0090.

Lake Oswego
Jenkins (Burlington)

In the heart of cranberry and blueberry farms, you will pass one of Rutgers University's Blueberry and Cranberry Field Research Stations on the left as you drive to Oswego Lake. Their barn-red buildings with white trim are somewhat of a landmark in the area. Hawks frequent the open fields, blue jays screech through the woods, and cardinals dart through the cedars. I've seen people fish here occasionally, but I've never seen anyone catch anything. There's a small clearing with picnic tables on a point of land east of the launch with a pretty view of the lake.

Cedar, sweet gum, and red maple line the waters within predominantly pine and oak lowland woods studded with American holly, hickory, and elder. Along the bank, look for the tiny, glossy-green leaves of the low-growing cranberry; its green fruit starts to turn red around the middle of August. If you visit in October and November, when the fruits are ripe, be aware that wild cranberries are quite tart. Ocean Spray has facilities near here to make the cranberry juice you buy in the supermarket. The blueberries, however, are sweet and ready to eat. When water levels are high, you can follow the Oswego River upstream from the eastern end of the lake for about 1.0 mile.

Facing the lake from the launch, look straight across and to the left; you'll see the small dam and a few tiny clearings to the right of the dam. During paddling season, local outfitters drop off kayak and canoe groups at the launch. They paddle across the lake, portage their boats over the narrow sand dike, and put in at the Oswego River for a three-hour paddle downstream to Harrisville Pond.

Touted as one of the prettiest rivers in the Pine Barrens, Oswego River takes you through Atlantic white cedar swamps, lowland forests, and freshwater marshes. If you want to combine biking and paddling, this is ideal. Lock your bike to a tree at the Harrisville landing, then

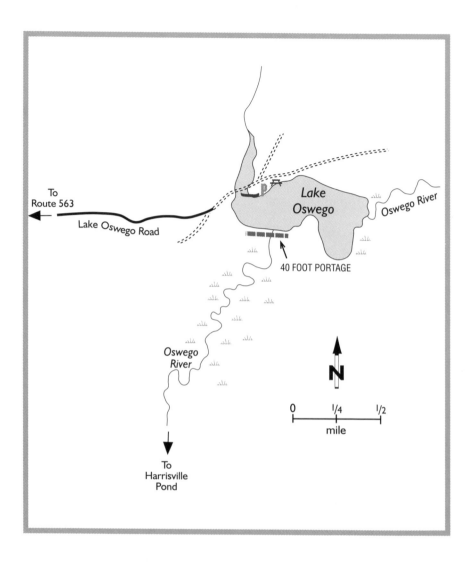

To
Route 563

Lake Oswego Road

Lake Oswego

Oswego River

40 FOOT PORTAGE

Oswego
River

N

0   1/4   1/2
mile

To
Harrisville
Pond

drive back to Oswego Lake. Paddle around the lake for a while and portage over the small sand dike to put in on the river.

When you arrive at Harrisville Pond, paddle to the landing beach and picnic area at the southern end on the right. The bike ride back to Oswego is an easy 5.0 miles, as the land is fairly flat. Since this is a prime biking location, an official bike lane has been designated along Route 679 for safer travel. More roads in the area are slated for similar lanes in the near future.

As you paddle in the heart of blueberry and cranberry country, look for the succulent wild berries along the shore.

Camping is available at Turtle Run Campground located right off Route 542, just 3.2 miles east of Route 563. Turtle Run Campground, P.O. Box 129, New Gretna, NJ 08224; 609-965-5343. Also see campgrounds listed under Batsto Lake.

Getting there

From Route 542, drive north 6.8 miles on Route 563, turn right onto Lake Oswego Road, and drive 3.4 miles to the launch site on the right, just past the guardrailed bridge going over a creek. The old blacktop portion of the road is bumpy and turns into a sand road near the end. A sign designating Penn State Forest will be on the right side of the road at the launch site.

Alternately, from Route 532, drive south 9.6 miles on Route 563 and turn left onto Lake Oswego Road. Proceed as above. Wharton State Forest, 4110 Nesco Road, Hammonton, NJ 08037; 609-561-0024.

Harrisville Pond
Harrisville (Burlington)

Wild blueberry bushes peek out among the cedar and pine dominating the shoreline of Harrisville Pond. Mountain and sheep laurel blossoms bring delicate touches of pink and white to the landscape in early summer, along with the white flowers of the lightly scented bog magnolia. In midsummer, the aroma of sweet pepperbush fills the air as cranberries begin to grow on its moist shores. Old cedar stumps in the large cove on the northwest end of the pond are perfect basking spots for turtles. If you feel energetic, you can paddle to its northeast corner, where the Oswego River enters, then paddle upstream for about

Picking wild blueberries for a tasty snack.

To Lake Oswego

Martha Pond

Route 563

Route 679

To Route 542

Oswego River

Harrisville Pond

P

P

N

Harrisville Forge Ruins

0   1/4   1/2
mile

Bodine Field Camping Area

1.0 mile. The first large cove on the right (east) as you paddle north becomes carpeted with yellow and white pond lilies in late summer.

This is a good opportunity to combine biking and hiking in the same outing by starting your trip on Lake Oswego. See details of the trip under Lake Oswego.

Getting there

From Route 542, drive north 5.4 miles on Route 563. Turn right (east) onto Route 670, and drive 1.4 miles to the launch site and picnic area on your left. Launch anywhere along the small beach. Parking is informal. Wharton State Forest, 4110 Nesco Road, Hammonton, NJ 08037; 609-561-0024.

Wilson Lake
Clayton (Gloucester)

Scotland Run Park on the southeast side of Clayton contains 900 acres of natural woodlands, hiking trails, and Wilson Lake. A small public beach with picnic tables, a playground, and restrooms occupies 300 feet of shoreline near the dam on the southwest end. Next to the concrete boat ramp, a fishing pier juts into the lake about 25 feet. Only electric motors are allowed, which makes for a quiet paddle. The majority of anglers cast their lines into the deeper waters near the dam for pickerel and smallmouth bass.

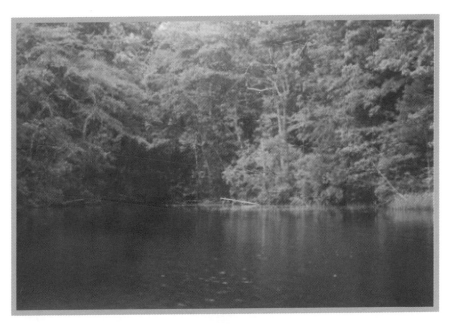

One of the many coves to explore on Wilson Lake.

A narrow hiking trail starts at the boat ramp along the north lakeshore and continues for 0.5 mile. The longer trail lies along the southern lakeshore and is accessible by foot or by landing on a small beach at 0.25 mile north of the dam. A few picnic tables are nestled in the nearby woods.

Most of the waters are shallow, averaging four feet, with deeper waters in the channel closer to the southern shore. Oak, pine, maple, and beech comprise the upland woods with cedar and red maple along the water's edge. Where aquatic vegetation approaches the surface, juvenile fish and a few species of turtles can be observed darting in and out of their protective environment.

On the northern end of the lake, where conditions more swamplike exist, cedar, magnolia, sweet gum, pickerelweed, and other water-loving flora dominate the landscape. Boglike coves and stump-strewn inlets create a perfect habitat for birds, turtles, deer, and raccoons. An abundant hawk population almost guarantees you'll see one while paddling—most likely the broad-winged hawk.

Getting There

From Route 610 (Clayton Road) on the southeast side of Clayton, drive 0.4 mile north on Route 655 (Fries Mill Road) to the park entrance on the right. Follow the signs to the boat launch. Portable toilets are located at the boat launch parking lot.

From Route 322, drive south 2.5 miles on Route 655 to the park entrance on the left. The nature center at Scotland Run Park sponsors nature lessons, monthly bird walks, and a kid's nature center, which meets once a month. Gloucester County Parks and Recreation, 6 Blackwood Barnsboro Road, Sewell, NJ 08080; 856-881-0845.

Lake Lenape
Mays Landing (Atlantic)

On its way to the Atlantic Ocean, the scenic Great Egg Harbor River was dammed to create Lake Lenape, most of which lies within the confines of Lake Lenape Park. Private property and the park's recreational facilities rim the southern end of the lake, but escape to wilder waters is an easy paddle away. The 1,900-acre park protects major portions of the Great Egg Harbor River, a nationally designated

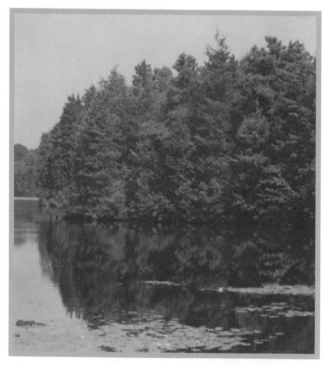

Lake Lenape along the Great Egg Harbor River, a nationally designated Wild and Scenic River.

N

0   1/2   1
mile

Route 559

Lake
Lenape

Mill Street

Route 50

To
Route 322

Route 559/
Old Harding Hwy.

Main Street
Route 40

Route 40

Route 40/50

Route 50

Wild and Scenic River. Campsites are available within the park, but they are not lakeside. A small fee is charged during the summer to enter the park.

Starting from the launch at Lake Lenape's southern tip, paddle northwest toward the headwaters. Along the way, sightsee around the many coves and explore deep inlets. Cedar lines the shores in front of mixed-oak and pine forests. Blueberry, sheep laurel, and mulberry bushes fill the understory, while stands of Phragmites and cattails grow in open shallows. After passing through the narrower central portion, the lake opens wide and beautiful. In the northwest corner, where the Great Egg Harbor River enters the lake, you can paddle upstream quite a few miles depending on the water level.

If you have children under 12, visit nearby Storybook Land, where kids can play in a village built around their favorite stories and classic nursery rhymes. Drive 7.4 miles east on Route 322 from Route 50 to the entrance on your right. Storybook Land, 6415 Route 322, Cardiff, NJ 08234; 609-646-0103.

Getting there

From Route 322 (Black Horse Pike), drive south 1.8 miles on Route 50. Turn right onto Main Street (Route 559) and drive 0.3 mile to the T. Turn left onto Mill Street (Route 559) for 0.1 mile, and then right onto Old Harding Highway (also Route 559) for 0.2 mile to the park entrance on your right. A concrete boat ramp is on the right just before the recreation center. Lake Lenape Park Recreation Center, 753 Park Road and 13th Street, P.O. Box 57, Mays Landing, NJ 08330; 609-625-2021 or 800-626-7612.

Lake Absegami
New Gretna (Burlington)

Lake Absegami lies in the northwest corner of the Bass River State Forest at the southern end of Burlington County. The 67-acre body of water offers cedar swamps, bogs, and pine and mixed-oak forests surrounding the tea-colored waters typical of the Pine Barrens. Large coves will provide hours of exploring as you discover something new

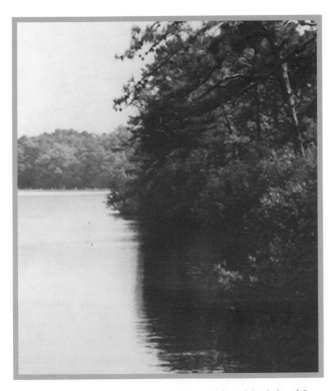

The cedar-lined shore provides enjoyable lakeside camping.

around each bend. Warblers, blue jays, cardinals, kingbirds, eastern pee-wees, and other songbirds add to the nature experience. While you're there, take advantage of camping in a tent, a lean-to, or a trailer within the pine-scented woodlands. The park also rents rustic cabins, a few of which are lakeside. Schedule your trip around a full moon cycle to enjoy a pleasant moonlight paddle before retiring. Playgrounds are located at the swimming beach and within the camping area.

Getting there

From southbound Garden State Parkway, take Exit 52 immediately after the tollbooth. Turn right onto East Greenbush Road (Route 654) at the end of the ramp and drive 1.1 miles to the T (Stage Road, but there's no sign). Turn right and drive 0.9 mile to the entrance of Bass River State Park on your left. After passing the booth (a fee is charged in summer), drive straight ahead to the sand boat-launch road on your left.

From northbound Garden State Parkway, take Exit 50 (Route 9). The ramp will cross back over the parkway and place you on Route 9 north. Drive 1.9 miles, turn left onto East Greenbush Road, and drive 0.8 mile to the T. Continue as above. Bass River State Forest, 762 Stage Road, P.O. Box 118, New Gretna, NJ 08224; 609-296-1114.

Corbin City Impoundments
Tuckahoe (Atlantic)

Get ready for great birding and remote, peaceful paddling. Impoundments, similar to shallow reservoirs, are large dammed areas creating basins to collect and confine waters. Three large impoundments, ranging from 104 to 284 acres, lie within the Lester G. MacNamara Wildlife Management Area not far from the Great Egg Harbor River. All offer spectacular scenery typical of lands bordering brackish marshes, where lowland woods stand behind the water-loving plants that frame creeks and ponds. Here you will find a mix of flora and fauna from freshwater and saltwater environments: hawks, muskrats, deer, fox, shorebirds, osprey, egrets, kingfishers, warblers, and numerous species of songbirds.

Sharing the waters with these elegant year-round residents.

Great Egg Harbor River

Griscom Mill Road

Route 50

Corbin City Impoundments

#3

dike

floodgate

floodgate

#2

dike

#1

floodgate

floodgate

floodgate

Griscom Mill Road

Route 49

To Garden State Parkway

N

0   1/2   1
mile

Kingfishers nest on the banks of the large islands in the middle impoundment.

While all three impoundments offer the nature lover spectacular opportunities, the southernmost impoundments offer a more adventurous trip, as you wind your way around numerous islands and into large coves. Kingfishers are most abundant in the second impoundment, where slightly steeper banks provide a better nesting habitat. Swans add a calm elegance, their snowy bodies contrasting against dark waters. Egrets and herons stalk the shallows everywhere, their long necks stretched out, searching for small fish swimming just beneath the surface. Don't forget your camera and lots of film for this trip. Electric outboards are permitted on the waters.

Camping is available at Scenic Riverview Campground in nearby Tuckahoe. Contact them at 465 Route 49, P.O. Box 184, Tuckahoe, NJ 08250; 609-628-4566. Take Route 50 south to Route 49 west and drive 2.5 miles. The entrance is on the right.

Getting there

Parking and launching are informal at best throughout the Wildlife Management Area. A few openings here and there through the narrow border of shrubs and trees rimming the impoundments provide access to the waters and enough widening in the road for a few cars to parallel park. Hug the edge when you park so as not to block other cars. Below are directions to some of the better launch spots. You're likely to find an angler or two pulled over to the side near the floodgate for each impoundment.

From Route 50 in Corbin City at the junction with Route 611 (Aetna Road), drive west 0.7 mile on Route 50 and turn right onto Griscom Mill Road. A sign for the Wildlife Management Area is on Route 50, but it is placed parallel to Route 50 and thus hard to see. After turning onto Griscom Mill Road, drive 0.4 mile to where the blacktop ends and a sand road begins. Continue another 1.6 miles, following the main sand road to the southern end of the south impoundment. There is room to park your car here and launch from the sandy embankment. For the next launch to the south impoundment, drive another 0.5 mile to a small clearing between the shrubs on the left.

For access to the middle impoundment: From above, continue another 0.3 mile to the right bend in the road, where you can launch into the southern end of the middle impoundment. Drive another 0.4 mile to another launch area—my favorite, as kingfishers are easy to spot here. Continue another 1.3 miles for access to the north impoundment. From that point, continue driving on the main sand road 2.2 miles to the junction of Route 50. You will be 3.5 miles farther north on Route 50 from where you started.

To get to Route 50 from the Garden State Parkway, take Exit 29 and turn west onto Route 623 (Roosevelt Boulevard). Drive 0.8 mile, following a curve to the left onto Route 631 (Tuckahoe Road). Drive 4.9 miles to its junction with Route 50. Turn right (west) onto Route 50 and continue as above. New Jersey Division of Fish and Wildlife, Southern Region, (Winslow WMA), 229 Blue Anchor Road, Sicklerville, NJ 08081; 856-629-0090.

Stewart Lake
Woodbury (Gloucester)

Stewart Lake's 45 acres are surrounded entirely by a municipal park. In some areas the woods thin, leaving only a modest screen between you and civilization; elsewhere they provide a thick blanket of insulation. Upland woods of maple, hickory, sassafras, tulip, ash, and pine delight you with splashes of red, orange, and yellow in fall and cool greens in summer. There's abundant wildlife to be found and attractive scenery that's easy on the eyes. Raccoons, possum, and skunk are more likely to be spotted on the thickly wooded northeast end near the boat launch,

Heavily wooded parklands grace the northern end of the lake near the boat ramp.

while turtles and frogs are more prevalent in shallow areas on the eastern banks. Only electric outboards are permitted, so it will be quiet on the water. Recreational facilities are centrally located on the north side of this horseshoe-shaped lake, but only the tree-studded picnic area is lakeside.

Getting there

From Route 534 (Good Intent Road), drive west 1.5 miles on Route 506 (Cooper Street). Slow after you pass under the turnpike bridge, as the entrance to the boat launch on the right comes up fast. Turn right into the boat launch area then park courteously (parking is limited).

There's an alternate launch location from the park's recreational site, where a large lakeside picnic grove and playground are provided. From Route 534 (Good Intent Road), drive west 2.3 miles on Route 506, turn right (north) onto Evergreen Street, and drive 1.2 miles, turning right onto Red Bank Avenue. Then drive 0.1 mile to the park's entrance on your right. Turn into the park, drive past the building on your right, then over to the right side of the rear parking lot, where you will see a sign for the boat launch at the head of a dirt road.

Parvin Lake and Thundergust Lake
Centerton (Salem)

More than 1,100 acres of Parvin State Park are yours to enjoy for paddling, camping, fishing, and hiking. Mountain laurel and dogwood lend a delicate scent to the air in late spring, as their blossoms open wide to splash the landscape with color. Seventeen miles of hiking trails lead you through sweetly scented Atlantic white cedar swamps, lowland and upland hardwood forests, and mixed oak-pine forests, typical of the Pine Barrens. The park is home to the state-threatened barred owl and the endangered swamp pink, whose pink blossoms in late spring stand atop two-foot stalks. When you visit the swamp, search for the

Looking down Parvin Lake from the boat launch facility.

carnivorous pitcher plant, which thrives in this moist, acidic environment. Bog and painted turtles are common in the swamps and around the lakes. Parvin State Park is noted as a hot spot for the spring migration of neotropical songbirds.

Two lakes within the park, 95-acre Parvin Lake and 21-acre Thundergust Lake, give you plenty of water in which to paddle. In addition to tent sites, the park offers one group campsite on an island and lakeside cabins along the shore at Thundergust Lake. July and August bring crowds, so make camping reservations well in advance, particularly if you want one of the lakeside cabins.

Getting there

From Route 77, drive east 6.0 miles on Route 540 to the entrance and the park office on your right. Signs are posted prominently along Route 540. If you do not stop at the park office, continue another 0.3 mile, turn right onto Parvin Mill Road, and drive 0.15 mile to the launch site on your right. Parvin State Park, 701 Almond Road, Pittsgrove, NJ 08318; 609-358-8616.

Appendix

Map Sources

Ramsey Outdoor Stores
1039 Route 46 West
Ledgewood, NJ 07852
973-584-7799

Around the World in Maps
1305 New York Avenue
Manasquan, NJ 08736
732-223-5899

TO OBTAIN FREE MAP INDEXES AND CATALOGS OR TO ORDER TOPOGRAPHICAL MAPS:

United States Geological Survey Information Services
P.O. Box 25286
Denver, CO 80225
888-275-8747 or 303-202-4700

TOPOGRAPHICAL MAPS WITH DETAILED HIKING TRAILS:

New York/New Jersey Trail Conference (NYNJTC)
232 Madison Avenue, No. 802
New York, NY 10016
Office hours: M–F 11:00 A.M.–5:30 P.M.
212-685-9699

Paddling Equipment and Technique

Gullion, Laurie. 1993. *The Canoeing and Kayaking Instruction Manual.* Springfield, VA: American Canoe Association.

Knapp, Andy. 2000. *The Optimum Kayak: How to Choose, Maintain, Repair, and Customize the Right Boat for You.* Camden, ME: Ragged Mountain Press.

Rowe, Ray. 1993. *Teach Yourself Canoeing: A Practical Introduction to Canoeing and Kayaking.* Lincolnwood, IL: NTC Publishing Group.

Protecting the Environment

Hampton, Bruce, and David Cole. 1995. *Soft Paths.* Mechanicsburg, PA: Stackpole Books.

McGiveny, Annette. 1998. *Leave No Trace: A Practical Guide to the New Wilderness Ethic.* Branson, MO: Mountaineers Books.

Meyer, Kathleen. 1994. *How to Shit in the Woods.* Berkeley, CA: Ten Speed Press.

Camping/Campgrounds

Daniel, Linda. 1986. *Kayak Cookery.* Guilford, CT: Globe Pequot Press. (I hope none of my friends discover I know about this book, they may expect gourmet meals.)

Getchell, Annie. 1995. *The Essential Outdoor Gear Manual.* Camden, ME: Ragged Mountain Press.

Harrison, David. 1995. *Kayak Camping.* New York: Hearst Books.

Kuhne, Cecil. 1999. *Kayak Touring and Camping.* Mechanicsburg, PA: Stackpole Books.

Woodall Publishing. 2000. *The Complete Guide to Campgrounds, RV Parks, Service Centers and Attractions; Mid-Atlantic Camping Guide.* Lake Forest, IL: Woodall Publishing Corp.

Taking the Kids Along

Harrison, David and Judy Harrison. 1990.*Canoe Tripping with Children.* Guilford, CT: Globe Pequot Press.

Woodson, Roger and Kimberley Woodson. 1995.*The Parent's Guide to Camping with Children.* Cincinnati: Betterway Books.

Useful Addresses and Phone Numbers

Appalachian Mountain Club
5 Joy Street
Boston, MA 02108
617-523-0636; www.outdoors.org
New York-North Jersey chapter
212-986-1430

Appalachian Mountain Club
Mohican Outdoor Center
50 Camp Road
Blairstown, NJ 07825-9655
908-362-5670

Green Acres Program
501 East State Street
Station Plaza Building 5, Ground Floor
Trenton, NJ 08609-1101
609-984-0500

New Jersey Audubon Society Headquarters
9 Hardscrabble Road
P.O. Box 126
Bernardsville, NJ 07924
908-204-8998

The Nature Conservancy
New Jersey Field Office
Elizabeth D. Kay Environmental Center
200 Pottersville Road
Chester, NJ 07930
908-879-7262

The Sierra Club
57 Mountain Avenue
Princeton, NJ 08540
609-924-3141

New Jersey Division of Fish and Wildlife
P.O. Box 400
Trenton, NJ 08625
609-292-2965

New Jersey Recreation and Parks Association
4 Griggstown Causeway
Princeton, NJ 08540
908-281-9212

New Jersey Division of Parks and Forestry
501 East State Street, P.O. Box 404
Trenton, NJ 08625
800-843-6420

FOR GENERAL INFORMATION ABOUT WILDLIFE MANAGEMENT AREAS:
Pequest Trout Hatchery and Natural Resource Education Center
605 Pequest Road
Oxford, NJ 07863
908-637-4125

Alphabetical Listing of Lakes, Ponds, and Reservoirs

About the Author

Kathy Kenley is a marine biologist with additional degrees in geology and creative writing. She started kayaking in 1966, and since then has explored and paddled lakes, ponds, rivers, and coastal marshes along the East Coast and as far away as Thailand and Fiji. She has competed on the national level in many kayak races, and occasionally leads guided tours for a local outfitter within the Pine Barrens of southern New Jersey. Her current focus is to help introduce older men and women to the world of paddling.

Kenley, an avid scuba diver and snorkeler, owned and operated her own charter dive boat for more than ten years, and holds a United States Coast Guard captain's license. Her numerous eclectic interests range from paleontology to art and anthropology. She is committed to protecting the environment, participating in waterway cleanups and carrying a trash bag in her boat to pick up discarded refuse.

About the Appalachian Mountain Club

Since 1876, the Appalachian Mountain Club has helped people experience the majesty and solitude of the Northeast outdoors. We offer outdoor skills workshops, guided trips, and lodging options for all levels of outdoor adventuring. Our conservation programs include trail maintenance, air and water quality research, and conservation advocacy work to preserve the special outdoor places we love and enjoy for future generations.

Join the Adventure!

Take a hike, ride a bike, paddle a canoe. We believe that people who enjoy breathing fresh air, climbing mountains, splashing in streams, and walking on trails have more fun and take better care of the outdoors. Join the fun today. Call 617-523-0636 for membership information.

Outdoor Adventures

From beginner backpacking to advanced backcountry skiing, we teach outdoor skills workshops to suit your interest and experience. If you prefer the company of others and skilled leaders, we also offer guided hiking and paddling trips. Our four outdoor education centers guarantee year-round adventures.

Huts, Lodges, and Visitor Centers

With accommodations throughout the Northeast, you don't have to travel to the ends of the earth to see nature's beauty and experience unique wilderness lodging. Accessible by car or on foot, our lodges and huts are perfect for families, couples, groups, and individuals.

Books and Maps

We can lead you to the best hiking, biking, skiing, and paddling destinations from Maine to North Carolina. With more than 50 books and maps published, we re your definitive resource for discovering wonderful outdoor places. For ordering information call 800-262-4455.

Check us out online at **www.outdoors.org** for lots of great information.

Appalachian Mountain Club
5 Joy Street
Boston, MA 02108-1490
617-523-0636

Leave No Trace

The Appalachian Mountain Club is a national educational partner of Leave No Trace, Inc., a nonprofit organization dedicated to promoting and inspiring responsible outdoor recreation through education, research, and partnerships. The Leave No Trace Program seeks to develop wildland ethics—ways in which people think and act in the outdoors to minimize their impacts on the areas they visit and to protect our natural resources for future enjoyment. Leave No Trace unites four federal land management agencies—the U.S. Forest Service, National Park Service, Bureau of Land Management, and U.S. Fish and Wildlife Service—with manufacturers, outdoor retailers, user groups, educators, organizations like the AMC and the National Outdoor Leadership School (NOLS), and individuals.

The Leave No Trace ethic is guided by these seven principles:

- Plan ahead and prepare.
- Travel and camp on durable surfaces.
- Dispose of waste properly.
- Leave what you find.
- Minimize campfire impacts.
- Respect wildlife.
- Be considerate of other visitors.

The AMC has joined NOLS—a recognized leader in wilderness education and a founding partner of Leave No Trace—as the only sole national providers of the Leave No Trace Master Educator course through 2004. The AMC offers this five-day course, designed especially for outdoor professionals and land managers, as well as the shorter two-day Leave No Trace Trainer course, at locations throughout the Northeast United States.

For Leave No Trace information and materials contact:

Leave No Trace, Inc.
P.O. Box 997
Boulder, CO 80306
800-332-4100
www.LNT.org

Notes